Strategies for Productivity

INTERNATIONAL PERSPECTIVES

Sponsored by
Japan Productivity Center

Introduction by
PAUL TIPPETT
American Motors Corporation

Asian Edition co-published
with the
Asian Productivity Organization, Tokyo

UNIPUB • New York

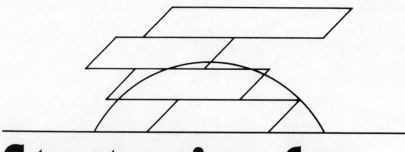

Strategies for Productivity

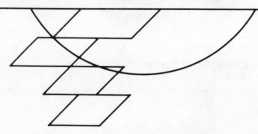

INTERNATIONAL PERSPECTIVES

Copyright © 1984 by UNIPUB

Library of Congress Cataloging in Publication Data

Main entry under title:

Strategies for productivity.

    Includes index.
    1. Industrial relations — Addresses, essays,
lectures. 2. Industrial productivity — Addresses,
essays, lectures. I. Nihon Seisansei Honbu.
HD6971.S87   1984   331   84-51511
ISBN 0-89059-034-6

Co-published in Asia by the
Asian Productivity Organization

Printed in the United States of America

84 85 86 87   9 8 7 6 5 4 3 2 1

Contents

A Rationale for Employment Security   31

GLENN E. WATTS

Employee–Management Relations in a Highly Unionized Environment   43

B. SVEDBERG

Labor–Management Relations in a New Technological Environment   51

SOICHIRO ASANO

PART 2

Productivity Measurement and Improvement

Productivity Scheme: A Case Study in Blue Circle Industries PLC   59

R. B. FREEMAN

PART 3

Productivity and the Japanese Corporation

Quality-Sustaining Competitiveness in the Japanese Auto Industry

TAKASHI ISHIHARA

The "Active" Firm: A Case Study of Nippon Kokan

MINORU KANAO

Contributors

Soichiro Asano
President, National Federation of Metal Industry Trade Unions; Vice Chairman, Japanese Private Sector Trade Union Council (JPTUC)

Thornton F. Bradshaw
Chairman of the Board and Chief Executive Officer, RCA Corporation; former President, Atlantic Richfield (then The Atlantic Refining Company); member, Board of Directors of Champion International, Security Pacific National Bank, and the Security Pacific Corporation; educated at Phillips Exeter Academy, Harvard College, and the Harvard Graduate School of Business Administration

Kenneth A. Charon
Group Director of Operations Planning, Information Systems and Communications Group, IBM Corporation; Vice President, Manufacturing, and earlier, Vice President of Administration and Information Systems, IBM Europe; B.A. degree, New York University, M.S. degree, Massachusetts Institute of Technology, Alfred P. Sloan Fellow, and graduate of the Northwestern University School of International Management

John T. Dunlop
Professor, Department of Economics, Harvard University, specializing in industrial relations; former U.S. Secretary of Labor (1975–1976)

R. B. Freeman
Manager, Group Personnel, Blue Circle Industries PLC; former Sales Manager, Prudential Assurance Company; currently charged with the PLC program for all

Blue Circle Industries' U.K. plants; Postgraduate Diploma in Management Services

Gene Gregory
Professor of International Business, Department of Comparative Culture, Sophia University; B.S. degree, Georgetown University School of Foreign Service; M.A. degree, Johns Hopkins School of Advanced International Studies

Takashi Ishihara
President, Nissan Motor Co., Ltd.; graduated from Law Department, Tohoku University

Minoru Kanao
President, Nippon Kokan KK; graduated from Department of Commerce, Waseda University

Ryoichi Kawai
Chairman, Komatsu Ltd.; graduated from Economics Department, Tokyo University; formerly with MITI

B. C. Roberts
Professor of Industrial Relations, London School of Economics and Political Science, University of London; former President, International Industrial Relations Association, former Visiting Professor, Princeton University, MIT, and University of California, Berkeley

B. Svedberg
President and Chief Executive Officer, Ericsson Telephone, Sweden; graduated from Royal Institute of Technology, Stockholm; attended Management Development Institute (IMEDE), University of Lausanne

Kotaro Tsujimura
Professor of Economics, Keio University, specializing in quantitative economics and economic policy

Glenn E. Watts
President, Communications Workers of America (CWA), membership of 508,000 (1979)

Foreword

Productivity can no longer be considered a domestic concern to be dealt with solely by industrialists, labor leaders, government officials, or business managers in a single country; it now transcends the national scope. The successful organizing of the International Productivity Symposium with its theme "Revitalizing the World Economy through Improved Productivity" clearly demonstrated this global interest and paramount need for productivity improvement and economic development.

The world is only beginning to recover from the global economic recession of the 1970s. While the productivity decline actually began for some nations in the 1960s, the shockwaves of the OPEC crude oil embargo rocked the foundations of the entire world economy. It caused a realignment of established price relationships among the factors of production—land, labor, capital, energy, and raw materials. Productivity growth suffered in all nations. The impact of declining productivity trends on the global standard of living began to be felt through most of the 1970s and early 1980s and affected national economic policies and international trade.

The symposium was thus timely in bringing together many leaders from around the world, each contributing to the spirit of international cooperation necessary to address worldwide productivity issues.

One of the assumptions made at the symposium was that in order to revitalize the world economy, countries must first activate their own economies through corporate vitality. While each nation has to work on productivity within its own traditions, culture, and institutions, productivity is no longer only a national concern: It is now a global concern.

Economies can no longer operate in total isolation from one another, and this shrinking world offers both opportunity and danger. We must find ways to cooperate so that each nation is producing products and services with its own greatest comparative advantage. If this is to occur, nations must learn from one another. This can best be done if nations come together to exchange ideas and thoughts about productivity. Instead of losing in the process, nations will gain. Nations sharing productivity information are entering not a win–lose but rather a win–win situation. This is the spirit the symposium promotes.

I would like to express appreciation to the Japan Productivity Center under the patronage of the Organization for Economic Cooperation and Development (OECD), the Japanese government, and supporting Japanese economic organizations and labor unions for their efforts in providing the Symposium as a vehicle to establish international cooperation in the field of productivity improvement and worldwide economic revitalization. And I encourage the continuation of the important dialogue initiated by this conference.

C. JACKSON GRAYSON, JR.
Chairman
American Productivity Center

Preface

The year 1985 marks the thirtieth anniversary of Japan's Productivity Movement since it was launched as an organized national campaign. Through these years, Japan's economy and industries have encountered and eventually overcome some serious difficulties.

Though the nation enjoyed a rapid economic growth in the early part of the period, it soon found itself facing stiffening resistance abroad against its expanding exports. Major international developments—such as the shift to floating foreign exchange rates and, above all, the OPEC oil crises—that sharply raised prices twice caused profound impact upon Japanese economy and society. These events and their impact indeed posed enormous challenges as well as severe tests for the Productivity Movement.

Since its establishment in 1955, the Japan Productivity Center has spearheaded the national movement under the three guiding principles: increased employment; cooperation and consultation between labor and management; and fair and equitable distribution of the fruits of improved productivity among management, labor, and the consumer. In pushing and promoting the movement, the Center set its goals and objectives to reflect changing needs and requirements of the times.

Today's industrial societies the world over commonly face fundamental issues such as the low-growth trend in their economies, an aging labor force, and rapid technological advances as exemplified in the field of electronics. The oil crises in the 1970s injected an element of extreme disharmony into the world economy, everywhere causing serious economic difficulties marked by stagnation and high unemployment.

Subsequent to discussions at the OECD Industry Committee in December, 1981, the International Productivity Symposium was held in Tokyo in May, 1983, under the sponsorship of the Japan Productivity Center to discuss ways to overcome the difficulties that began in the 1970s, as well as ways to revitalize the world economy through further productivity improvements. Various issues addressed by the symposium included measures that can be taken by corporate management to enhance productivity further, ways to effect better labor–management relations, and innovative approaches to cope with a changing economic and social environment.

Although the symposium's achievements may be many, I wish to note as a matter of extreme significance that the participants came to the common recognition that true productivity improvement and business revitalization can be achieved only when balanced and coordinated efforts and progress are made in both "hard" factors such as the introduction of new technology and advanced production equipment, and "soft" human elements of business such as labor–management relations and management organization. I am firmly convinced that this indeed constitutes a basic precept as we strive toward a better world economy of tomorrow.

This publication compiled from the proceedings of the symposium—the first of its kind ever held in the world—is an attempt to show various ways to achieve further productivity increase and "rejuvenate" business management in today's industrial world. I believe this is a timely undertaking, particularly in view of the ever-increasing degree of interdependence recognized among national economies and the ever-present needs for better understanding and stronger cooperation among nations in their common, long-term interests.

I wish to take this occasion to express my sincere appreciation to those panelists, contributors, and other participants in the symposium, without whose enthusiasm, active cooperation, and support such a volume would not have been possible. On behalf of the Japan Productivity Center, I also wish to reaffirm our commitment to continued efforts to contribute further to international productivity improvement.

KOHEI GOSHI
Chairman
Japan Productivity Center

Introduction

Surveying the wreckage of Japan's economy and industrial base in 1945, General Douglas MacArthur reportedly remarked that it would take eight Japanese workers to achieve the productivity of a single American worker. An executive from Japan's auto industry at the time went even further than the General and put the ratio at ten to one.

While those observations appear both amusing and ironic at this time, they are also a strong statement about the nature of productivity itself. Neither General MacArthur nor the Japanese executive was talking about differences in "how hard" Japanese and Americans worked. Rather, they were talking about the tools—managerial as well as physical—each worker had available. Japan's retooling and its mastery of adapting to its own product design and manufacturing techniques the innovations learned from the West in the decades after World War II is perhaps the greatest economic success story of our time.

Unfortunately, when most Americans finally became aware of what Japan had been doing to become more productive and competitive—by comparing the quality and prices of Japanese and U.S. television sets or seeing the impact of Japanese automobiles and steel on U.S. industry—the reaction was at times emotional, if not irrational. Throughout the 1970s, television documentaries and even some allegedly scholarly research on the so-called Japanese invasion focused not on the retooling and aggressive trade and industrial policies implemented by Japan after World War II (when the U.S. tended to rest on the laurels of its wartime tooling to convert to the production and export of consumer goods) but rather on alleged differences in psyches and attitudes of Japanese and American labor and management.

The key to Japan's productivity was too often seen not as a matter of incorporating state-of-the-art technology with a *pragmatic* attitude of worker–management cooperation but rather the mystical cultural differences between Japanese and American workers and managers. Americans were bombarded with images of smiling Japanese factory workers and executives lined up side by side, singing the company anthem, wearing the company uniform, strolling in the company park, and living in the company town.

Eventually there was even a debate as to whether the work ethic itself was in danger of disappearing in the U.S. and whether the individualistic, cantankerous American could ever hope to be as productive as his Japanese counterpart.

What a far cry from the world of General MacArthur and the Japanese executive of 1945!

The United States National Center for Productivity concluded in 1979 that if Americans were merely to sustain the standard of living they enjoyed in 1978, output per man-hour in manufacturing jobs would have to increase three percent a year in the 1980s. The total work force itself, however, is expected to increase only *one* percent a year in this decade, because of declining birth rates back in the 1960s. Therefore, industry will have to be more productive with fewer workers.

How then do we meet this new productivity challenge?

The solution, as the Japanese saw in 1945, is not to try to emulate a foreign culture. Nor is it to try to work ''harder,'' but rather to work ''smarter.'' Working smarter has always been the key to improved productivity.

During the past century, the average work week in the U.S. has been reduced from 70 to 40 hours—and in some cases less than 40 hours. At the same time, both real wages and overall productivity managed to increase. The U.S. achieved such progress not because it had discovered a supervitamin to make workers exert themselves more, but because new equipment and technology were developed and implemented to make production more efficient.

Today, the key to enhanced productivity lies not in somehow getting more work out of employees but in stimulating capital formation and R&D: in order to give the workers the tools to do a more efficient job. This is the area where basic manufacturing industries in Japan excelled and where the U.S. often lagged in the two decades after World War II.

However, in today's interdependent and competitive world market, meeting the challenge requires more than just retooling and dedication to R&D on the part of individual companies and industries. It requires cohesive national fiscal and trade policies.

Capital cannot be generated for tooling and R&D if interest rates are at prohibitively high levels, and prices for manufactured goods cannot be competitive with those from competing countries if the dollar is overvalued and other currencies undervalued. United States industry has made progress in improving its productivity (as was revealed in the Japan Productivity Center's international symposium) but there is still much to be done on this front of government fiscal and trade policy.

Despite the popular skepticism of a few years ago, the work ethic itself is alive in America today. As Studs Terkel found when he conducted his interviews for the book *Working* (Pantheon, New York, 1974), people continue to subscribe to the theory that the grass is greener on the far side of the hill. However, he also found that people still take pride in what they are doing on their own side of the hill and do not necessarily want to move to the other side.

Public opinion research continues to show that the American worker is just as dedicated and takes just as much pride in his work as does his counterpart in any country. Indeed, one survey of worker attitudes at a Nissan auto assembly plant near Tokyo and at American Motors' plant at Kenosha, Wisconsin, showed that American workers were more satisfied with many aspects of their jobs than were their Japanese counterparts. This survey was conducted in 1981 by the prestigious Nikko Research Center, based in Tokyo. AMC is also currently participating in an international study of the work ethic being conducted by the Japan Productivity Center in Europe, the U.S., and Japan.

Results of the kind of cross-cultural dialogue and analysis sponsored by the United States National Center for Productivity and the Japan Productivity Center show that neither country has an irreversible edge or unbeatable secret weapon when it comes to productivity. Japanese companies can continue to gain from some aspects of U.S. labor and management practices, just as U.S. companies have already learned from many aspects of Japanese practices.

The Japanese innovations of quality circles and the *kanban* "just-in-time" inventory control system, for example, are widely used in American industry today. American Motors uses just-in-time supply and shipping for more than one-third of all the parts used in its Renault Alliance and Encore passenger cars. Parts from 37 different suppliers are shipped distances ranging from 50 to 1000 miles on an as-needed basis, reducing inventory costs and allowing AMC to make more efficient use of plant space. AMC has also reduced the number of management layers separating the chief executive officer from the factory worker, in the pattern of the Japanese auto industry.

Looking across the Atlantic rather than the Pacific to the quality control system of its partner Renault, the French automaker, AMC has also adopted one of the most rigorous quality control audit systems in the auto industry. This audit is called AQR—"Action, Quality, Results." More than 600 items are checked in a process that takes two-and-one-half hours per vehicle.

To reinforce the essential principle that quality control is something that goes *into* the product rather than a mechanism to catch errors once the product leaves the assembly line, the teams conducting these quality audits are rotated so that each worker in the plant participates. After each audit, a "quality corner" session is held. Each worker discusses the problems discovered in the audit and ways to reduce and eliminate them in the manufacturing process.

To reinforce further each worker's appreciation of the importance of his individual contribution, AMC has gone beyond the Japanese concept of quality circles and established a program called ''Talk to the Boss about Quality,'' with a hot line telephone accessible to each worker. A study team organized by the Japan Productivity Center from five Japanese companies was sufficiently impressed with this innovation to take photographs and written reports back to Japan after touring the AMC plant in Kenosha, Wisconsin, earlier this year.

Again, there is no monopoly on productivity or innovation. There is much that Americans can learn from the Japanese, and vice versa. This is one of the strongest themes emerging from the Japan Productivity Center's First International Productivity Symposium. I am confident that when the next symposium convenes in Germany in 1986, even more common ground for progress will be unearthed.

PAUL TIPPETT

Chairman and Chief Executive Officer
American Motors Corporation

PART 1

Labor Relations
and Corporate Goals

The Challenge of Planning Corporate Strategy

THORNTON F. BRADSHAW

Chairman of the Board and Chief Executive Officer
RCA Corporation
United States

For so long, the world economy seemed to be going well. Countries had recovered from the devastation of the big war. Some, in fact, had performed miracles of industrial progress—Japan among them. Other industrialized nations were growing richer and richer, their citizens enjoying higher and higher standards of living. Nonindustrialized countries began to have hope, although many newly independent countries had to spend an inordinate amount of time on political problems rather than economic growth. And then the great industrial machine of the world began to falter, to run out of steam.

Few countries escaped the dislocations that plagued the world economies, whose interdependence grew strikingly apparent. In the U.S. we entered into the most severe recession since the great depression of the 1930s. In our battle to contain inflation (which we have only temporarily won), unemployment boiled over. The U.S. has become less competitive abroad—selling in the world markets—and at home—selling to the people of the U.S. More importantly, this loss of competitiveness appears to be centered in the very industries that had provided the growth of real wealth in the U.S. in the past.

It is difficult to identify which industries will take the place of the great wealth producers of the past. If in truth the U.S. will no longer be steelmakers to the world, what will it provide?

And so we come to strategic planning. Can business plan its way out of the present difficulties? Businessmen have already laid the foundations and built the plants—they are reluctant to plan to go out of business. Thus the first point is this: don't expect too much of corporate strategic planning, particularly in the context of the larger issues under discussion here. Business doesn't like to plan to discontinue products that have been successful in the past. The second point: as the businessman's world becomes larger, as his local market expands to a world market, his ability to influence that larger world decreases. The price of oil has

3

been and still is set by a cartel of oil-producing countries. While it may be possible for a company to forecast the price of oil, although difficult, it is surely not possible for a businessman to influence the price of oil.

In this broader arena only governments can plan and only governments can take action. However, there are wide variations among governments. The U.S. government is notoriously reluctant to plan, while other nations are reluctant to leave anything to the sloppiness of the marketplace. Yet the American businessman is expected to plan his way to international prosperity in this changing mixture of mixed economies.

No wonder corporate strategy has a bad name. We are often wrong and probably for the reasons mentioned. First, we are reluctant to plan our way out of our main line businesses; second, so much planning can be consigned to the wastebasket by the flick of a pen by a prime minister here or a president there. Finally, as someone has said, forecasting is a risky business, particularly forecasting the future.

A few good things about corporate strategic planning should be said. I have spent a good deal of my life thinking about and doing something about corporate strategic planning, first as a professor at Harvard, then as a management consultant, then as the president of an oil company, then as the chairman of an electronics company. I have never regretted the expenditure of any of this time even when I was wrong, which was a lot of the time.

Strategic planning is a continuing search for identity. Every company must know what it is as well as what it intends to be—or else suffer the consequences. If management does not know what the company is about, then it is a good bet that investors don't know and sources of funds dry up. If employees don't know, then morale dries up. If customers don't know, then the business dries up. The very act of planning for the future and searching for ways to communicate those plans to people inside and outside the company keeps this constant and essential search for identity in motion. The process also keeps a company trim and fit. If the planning process goes on continuously, as it should, it is just like doing daily exercises—sometimes dull, sometimes repetitive, but all in all they do make the body (corporate or individual) more trim, more flexible, more ready to move fast when the time comes.

Having said a few things about the limitations of corporate strategic planning and a few reasons why no company should be without it, some actual planning experiences may underscore these points. In 1964, Robert Anderson became the chairman and I became the president of the Atlantic Refining Company, which later became the Atlantic Richfield Company. While traveling together, we enumerated six objectives for the company on the back of an airline menu. These objectives were never forgotten.

First, the company refined and marketed more products than it could supply with its own crude oil. It existed at the whim of the crude oil market and was subject to large swings in profit. Therefore, the first objective was to bring the company into balance—find more crude oil.

Second, the marketing and refining segments of the business were losing money and had been for many years. Objective number two was to bring this part of the business into a profit status standing on its own.

Third, our petrochemical business was so small that it scarcely existed. We knew that the highest end use value for hydrocarbons was in petrochemicals. The third objective was to build the petrochemical business.

Fourth, we had very little foreign crude oil and little chance of competing with the great major oil companies. The fourth objective was more of a negative one—it was not to become an international oil company but to play the foreign exploratory field on an ad hoc opportunity basis. If we could make money with an Iranian or an Indonesian play, we would go for it.

Fifth, we knew that the age of oil and gas would not last forever. Hydrocarbons take millions of years to be created and we were using them up at a great rate. Our fifth objective was therefore to become involved in alternative energy sources—coal, shale, tar sands, nuclear energy, solar energy.

Sixth, and finally, since there was pressure by the government at that time to keep oil companies out of the alternative energy source business, a diversification program seemed the best hedge. In terms of our skills and experience, diversification into hard metals became the sixth and final objective.

These objectives became the gospel at Atlantic Richfield almost 20 years ago and still are today. Atlantic Richfield is now the tenth largest industrial company in the U.S., with annual profits of about $1.6 billion. When that list was drawn up, it was a very small regional oil company with profits of about $35 million and was scarcely considered a worthy competitor.

Today, Atlantic Richfield is in balance (its first objective)—its own crude oil is equal to its refining and marketing capacity; its marketing and refining operation is profitable on its own; its petrochemical business is very large, with sales of several billion dollars; it is not an international oil company although it has made money through international oil plays; it has a very large position in coal and solar energy and has been in and out of nuclear energy, tar sands, and shale; finally, Atlantic Richfield is a major factor in copper, aluminum, brass, and other hard minerals.

All this did not happen merely because the objectives were listed, but they could not have happened if the company did not know its strengths and weaknesses and have a clear idea of what kind of a company it could become. And it could not have happened if we had not stuck with it.

Of course, finding the giant Prudhoe Bay oil field helped. But that was objective number one—look for domestic crude oil. We would not have found it if we had not been looking. And, of course, we didn't just post the list of objectives on the bulletin board. We rebuilt the corporate planning department.

We used the six points as basic doctrine, but we knew that chapter headings do not make a book. The changes, the flexibility, the detail, the implementation plans, all had to come from the entire organization, orchestrated by the planning department.

One other aspect of planning emerges from this particular experience. The government writes what the bill of fare is to be and, of course, can change it at will. During the 1960s and much of the 1970s, the U.S. government believed that we did not as a nation have to plan for supplies of energy and, in fact, that cheap energy could be legislated by setting prices. Both these policies—hands off business and hold energy prices below costs—were very popular—not very effective, but very popular.

A great deal of corporate planning effort in the Atlantic Richfield Company during the 1970s was devoted to developing national energy policies and then trying to sell them—to the media, to the people, and finally to the politicians. Eventually it worked. The U.S. did recognize that without energy it could not remain an industrialized nation, that energy had to be planned for, and that the government had a very large responsibility to lead the way in planning for adequate energy supplies. In the late 1970s, the U.S. did join the rest of the world in adopting an energy policy.

This final point is a most crucial problem and a most vexing one. Business and government in all of our countries are so intertwined that planning in one area without consideration of the other is totally impossible. And yet, in some countries, private businessmen are supposed to plan; the government is not supposed to plan industrial matters. In other countries, the government plans and businessmen cooperate. These differences are basically at the heart of our difficulties in reaching understanding of our trade problems.

My experience at RCA corresponds to the genesis of the six points, to the building of a planning process within the company, and to the participation in the development of government policy. RCA did not have a president when I became chairman, but it was not at all difficult to sense the general directions of the planning process. Setting directions merely means lining up present strengths with future market opportunities. It does no good for a company to have a work force trained and competent in making buggy whips if the market for buggy whips is declining. Having engineers within a company at the leading edge of laser technology is a different matter entirely.

When I joined RCA, I found the innovative core of the company to be intact. The great David Sarnoff Laboratories had not been starved for funds; indeed, they had been fed more and more each year, until last year the innovators in the laboratories produced more patents than at any other laboratory except General Electric.

The billions of dollars of systems work done for the government each year consisted of some of the most sophisticated and advanced scientific work being done in the U.S. RCA was manufacturing and selling more color television sets than any other company in the U.S. market and its quality was second to none. The marketing structure for consumer electronics was exceptionally strong; RCA could and did build the number one position in videocassette recorders in the U.S. even though it had to import these VCRs. Its service company structure spanning the entire U.S. was exceptionally strong and was used to service not only RCA products but those of other companies. RCA had been a pioneer in the building and operation of satellites and had achieved the number one position in the world. The capacity for innovative programming at NBC and the tradition and practice of good news gathering and presentation had not declined and was ready for the next steps forward.

Behind these strengths were finely trained people and a large tradition. On this basis, it was not hard to set forth the proper objectives list—electronics, communications, entertainment, and information. It so happened that the timing was right. An electronics revolution built on the transistor is sweeping the world. A communications revolution built on the satellite and the semiconductor is also transforming the world. Both of these changes in technologies have produced and are still producing new information delivery systems, some whose outlines can only dimly be perceived. Whatever form they take, they will need to be fed—with information and entertainment. The future will be different, and electronics, communications, and information will make it different.

Electronics, communications, and entertainment bring RCA back to its roots, to its real identity, to its areas of concentration, and in that sense it is as significant as the Atlantic Richfield Company's six points of almost 20 years ago. Here again, as in the case of the Atlantic Richfield Company, it is not enough to set the general directions and then wait for results to pour in. The entire organization has to become a part of the planning process and then the action program. Furthermore, setting broad general goals, or parameters—electronics, communications, entertainment—raises more questions than it answers. What kind of electronics? The world of electronics is very broad—we can't cover it all and have no intention of trying. After all, we have to leave something for Matsushita, Philips, and General Electric. In communications, there are companies who do some things far better than we ever could—AT&T, IBM, ITT. I doubt if we would want to compete directly with the great movie studios in producing feature films, and so there are questions of which specific main product lines and which specific niches to aim at.

There are also questions of where to place our bets for developments of the future. All of the electronic delivery systems are not going to win; only some. Neither are all the entertainment programs for the future going to win. We have already had some experience with that. Organization and processes already set in place and in motion will help draw forth answers from the entire company. The objective of the planning process remains the same as it was in the Atlantic

Richfield case—to ensure that bottom-up planning meets top-down planning and that each reinforces the other during the entire process. It is like building a bridge from two sides of a river—the engineers have to work together from the beginning if the idea is to create one bridge that joins in the middle.

One of the lessons learned at Atlantic Richfield was that corporate planning may be a useful exercise, but it is a fruitless one if the government changes the rules of the game. The development of a national energy policy, for instance, was the most crucial element in any energy company's planning.

What is the U.S. government's bill of fare for the electronics industry? I do not believe it has been written yet, and I am hopeful that it will not be—at least until we have worked our way through some of our present trading and monetary difficulties. In spite of a number of recent actions, the U.S. government remains committed to the principles of free trade and a minimum of government intervention in the affairs of private companies. The definition of "minimum intervention" has changed quite drastically in recent years. Yet I would not like to see our government change this general attitude toward a minimum of political intervention, particularly in the area of international trade. Neither would RCA, which has championed free trade for many years.

On the other hand, the pressures for protectionism are growing in the U.S. and could reach dangerous proportions. Our high unemployment rate, the displacement of some of our basic industries, some of the procedural difficulties we face in the world trade arena, and monetary policies, all seem to have combined to produce a good deal of noise and some action, which indicate that full-fledged protectionism is once again becoming a political rallying point.

No single change in U.S. policy is likely to do more harm to economic recovery in the U.S., and indeed in the world, than a return to protectionism among the industrialized nations. What can private businessmen do to prevent this? What can we do to assure that we can carry through with strategic planning that will result in improved standards of living throughout the world? There are a number of things. I will suggest only one. I am not an expert on international money matters, but I do know this: the present distortion in currency values has made it nearly impossible for companies to plan ahead and is probably contributing to the delay in worldwide economic recovery and undoubtedly fueling the fires of protectionism.

More than a decade ago, the Bretton Woods Agreement was replaced by a system of floating exchange rates. Currency became dependent on internal monetary policies and not upon international policy or agreement. Exchange rates no longer reflect the competitive strengths of the industries of the various nations. Vast amounts of currencies now move, not only in payment of goods but seeking investment or merely as speculation. This means that the competitive value of a product can be changed in a very short time—without anything "real" happening. This also means that a manufacturer cannot plan to introduce a new product outside his own country a few years down the road and have any idea of what the price will be or whether the product will be competitive.

My colleague—and esteemed competitor—Akio Morita, chairman of Sony, addressed this problem recently. The solution he said, "is to establish exchange rates that match the industrial strengths of our various nations. Then we can propose that American automobiles and Japanese automobiles (or television sets) compete on this basis, with the final arbiter being the general public (or marketplace)." I support Mr. Morita's proposal. I hope that the major nations of the world will recognize that a stable currency is vital to economic growth and to free trade. Creation of some form of coordinated monetary policy would be an effective deterrent to the protectionist tide that threatens free trade. Such a system would allow goods to be judged competitively and fairly—and not by fluctuating exchange rates.

In the 1970s, I fought for a U.S. energy policy coordinated with the energy policies of other nations. Now, I should like to fight for a coordinated monetary policy to provide a new and stronger base for free trade among nations. This is included in RCA's strategic plan. I hope you will consider including it in yours.

Labor Organization, Markets, and Economic Vitalization

JOHN T. DUNLOP

Lamont University Professor
Harvard University
United States

Markets do not exist in some conceptual or disembodied form; rather, they take various institutional shapes among which there is considerable variation. Actual markets do not operate as some abstract or idealized model: institutional arrangements are shaped by buyers and sellers, cultural factors, international trade and financial influences, and a variety of governmental policies. Economic vitality is much influenced by these institutional forms in various markets, e.g., labor markets, raw material markets, product markets, financial markets, and markets for new technologies and ideas.

MARKETS AND THEIR INSTITUTIONS

From the outset of economic analysis, it has been recognized that certain basic institutional arrangements are essential to a modern market system:[1] the right to contract to buy and sell, a money and financial system, the absence of a hereditary caste system or slavery in the labor market, government order, and a legal system that precludes expropriation and wanton banditry.

However, when we stress the significance of the institutional forms of markets, we also refer to more technical and detailed features of markets that affect their performance. Institutional factors will determine barriers set by regulation for entry: licensure or standards other than those set by economies of scale or costs; the flow of information available to potential buyers or sellers; the dimensions of the transactions—such as price, quality, grades, delivery, required approvals—that may significantly affect a transaction; conventions on frequency

---

[1]See the formulation of Frank H. Knight, *The Ethics of Competition and Other Essays*, New York: Augustus M. Kelley, Inc., 1935, pp. 41–75.

of price quotations or changes; and regulations such as antitrust affecting the interactions of buyers and sellers. These and other features of a market will clearly influence the terms of transactions between buyers and sellers and other measures of the performance of a market.[2]

Consider the institutional features involved in the labor market, referring in general terms to those in the U.S. Fundamentally, the labor market is not a bourse where an auction clears the market regularly, say, on a daily or weekly basis.[3] The labor market brings together different enterprise buyers and different sellers of labor. Apart from labor organizations or regulation, any differing social views of workers and managers as to what is fair and equitable can have significant effects on labor market behavior. Any view of the labor market is required to recognize the rules relating to patterns of movements in internal labor markets, i.e., administrative units in which rules rather than market forces determine promotions, transfers, temporary and permanent layoffs, hiring sequences, retirements, etc.[4] If we consider government regulations (federal, state, or local) relating to minimum wages, unemployment insurance, age discrimination, health and safety, accidents and disability and related compensation, retirement and pensions, etc., a vast complex of labor market regulations is apparent. To this we must add the broad spectrum of training and educational institutions that essentially are uncoordinated to labor markets and largely pursue their own objectives. In addition to these different labor market institutions and practices, we also have the creations of imaginative management and of collective bargaining policies.

The purpose of this recital of different features and institutional forms of labor markets is to underscore two observations:

(1) Labor market institutions are not standardized. They are enormously diverse and it is not easy to generalize about them.

(2) The intervention of public policy in our country is not coordinated; it does not accord with or respond to any master plan or overall public policy toward labor markets, or for that matter toward any other markets. Government policy or intervention does not impact at one point, but is striated through labor markets, administered by different agencies and levels of government, uncoordinated and at times mutually inconsistent and conflicting. There is no mechanism or policy

---

[2]See F. M. Scherer, *Industrial Market Structure and Economic Performance*, Chicago: Rand McNally, 1971.

[3]John T. Dunlop, *Wage Determination Under Trade Unions*, New York: Macmillan, 1944, pp. 11, 118.

[4]John T. Dunlop, "Job Vacancy Measures and Economic Analysis" in *The Measurement of Job Vacancies*, National Bureau of Economic Research, New York: Columbia University Press, 1966, pp. 32–38. Peter B. Doeringer and Michael J. Piore, *Internal Labor Markets and Manpower Analysis*, Lexington, Mass.: Heath Lexington Books, 1971.

for interaction or a coordinated approach between the public and the private sectors.

The institutional arrangements regarding government regulation of financial and product markets, just as observed with respect to labor markets, are decisive to their performance. The standards for admission or license to the activity, the process for access to information regarding the intentions of buyers and sellers, the numerous dimensions of products and services, the length of time required for buyers and sellers to have effects upon price and other dimensions of scale, and the various strands of regulation that intersect a financial or product market are all essential ingredients of these markets.

The simple, yet fundamental, observation is that there is no abstract entity called a market apart from its institutional setting. The institutional complex of a market, including associated regulations, shapes the performance of the market and gives meaning to the concept of ''market competition.'' These considerations are not readily compressed into an instantaneous demand and supply function.

Thus far, the discussion of markets and their institutions requires a recognition that markets—be they labor, financial, or products markets—are not isolated and independent and that they and their institutions interact one on the other.[5] For the enterprise, products and factors compete one with the other and, to certain degrees, are substitutes one for the other. As I have emphasized over the last 40 years with regard to labor organization policies, changes in product market competitive conditions influence related labor markets, and changes in labor markets affect competition in related product markets. The recent experience in the U.S. with deregulation of trucking freight rates by the Interstate Commerce Commission and its adverse effects upon wages and conditions of trucking employees under collective agreements is only the latest illustration of this interdependence.

THE DEBATE ON THE CONSEQUENCES OF LABOR ORGANIZATIONS

For more than 150 years, economists have debated the consequences of labor organizations and government regulation of labor markets on other markets and upon performance of the economy. In the past 30 years the econometric measurement of the consequences of labor organizations has become a popular academic pursuit in the U.S. In general, the classical English economists were strongly in

---

[5]See Kotaro Toujimura, Masahiro Kuroda, and Haruo Shimada, *Economic Policy and General Interdependence,* Tokyo: Kogakusha Ltd., 1981.

favor of the liberty of association of wage earners and after the war with Napoleon, none were more forward to agitate for the repeal of laws that prohibited the combination of wage earners. However, as Lionel Robbins also points out, "a profound unease and uncertainty dominates the work of the later classical economists" confronted with problems associated with labor organizations, such as strikes, violence, and disorder.[6]

The subsequent judgment of Alfred Marshall must clearly be regarded as relatively favorable. He emphasized that "with freedom [of association] came responsibility."[7] He stated that the chief aims of unions are generally "the increase in wages, the reduction in hours of labour, the securing healthy, safe and pleasant conditions of work, and the defending individual workers from arbitrary and unjust treatment by their employers" as well as granting "provident benefits to members in need."[7] Marshall believed that for his day the strongest argument that unions increased the national dividend derived from their effects "on the character of the workers themselves,"[8] giving members a new spirit and a trust in and care for one another and "inciting them to avail themselves of those economic forces that can be made to work on their side."[9]

On the other hand, the line of economists holding that labor organizations and collective bargaining have serious adverse effects upon the national economy include such writers of the past generation as Henry Simons, Fritz Machlup, and Edward H. Chamberlin, to name only a few of the more outspoken.

It may be useful to discuss briefly the principal contending elements of the views that reach such opposing economic judgments on the consequences of labor organizations for the economy. One central problem needs to be identified in comparing these arguments. Those who consider the impact of labor organizations to be relatively favorable tend to compare the consequences of collective bargaining with nonunion and unorganized conditions, while those impressed with the negative consequences of labor organizations tend to compare the consequences of collective bargaining with idealized competitive markets or some other competitive model rather than with actual nonunion conditions. Accordingly, the contending positions often do not appropriately confront each other.

(a) *Less productive versus more productive work places.* Those who hold that labor organizations increase productivity emphasize (1) the role of apprenticeship and improved training, (2) an improvement in the morale of the work force or "fostering habits of sobriety, honesty, independence and self-respect,"

---

[6]Lionel Robbins, *The Theory of Economic Policy in English Classical Political Economy,* London: Macmillan, 1953, pp. 106–110.

[7]Alfred Marshall, *Elements of Economics of Industry,* London: Macmillan, 1893, p. 375. (See Book VI, Chapter XIII.)

[8]*Ibid.,* p. 400.

[9]*Ibid.,* pp. 401–402.

to use Marshall's language, (3) an improvement in the quality of health and safety of the workplace, (4) an improvement in the quality of management. As Sumner H. Slichter concluded in a lifetime of study, "The challenge that unions presented to management, if viewed broadly, created superior and better balanced management, even though some exceptions must be recognized."[10] Reference needs to be made to the limited number of workplaces and collective bargaining relationships, at least in the U.S., where highly cooperative productive programs are in operation, i.e., the relatively few quality circles and labor–management committees.

Against this affirmative view of labor organizations, the argument is that unions lead to inefficient work rules and artificial restraints on management that inhibit productivity. The formal argument of Machlup, "If we assume that capital is scarce and labor fully employed, the substitution of capital for labor in the industries in which wage rates are raised can mean only one thing: the availability of less capital and more labor in all other fields of economic activity. The result may be unemployment of labor or reallocation of labor with more labor employed in fields where it can be employed only with reduced productivity."[11] He concludes that there is "no support for the argument that forced wage increases can be paid out of a wage-boost–induced increase in labor productivity."[12]

(b) *Continuing strife and violence versus orderly dispute resolution.* Marshall believed that the attention to strikes had been exaggerated and that machinery to resolve disputes, particularly in industries involved in foreign trade, was a significant contribution of labor organizations. Moreover, he understood that to resolve disputes effectively a union needed to have internal strength. "Little but mischief indeed comes from a weak Union, always ready to interfere, but seldom able to secure the faithful carrying out of an agreement."[13] From a long-term perspective it can also be observed that as industrial relations systems develop, more formalized systems of dispute resolution also emerge, and violence, including death in labor disputes, and work stoppages become far less frequent or serious.[14]

Against these views is the judgment, expressed most often after a period of large-scale strikes, that work stoppages are a major fault of unions and adversely

---

[10]Sumner H. Slichter, James J. Healy, and E. Robert Livernash, *The Impact of Collective Bargaining on Management,* Washington, D.C.: The Brookings Institution, 1960, p. 951.

[11]Fritz Machlup, *The Political Economy of Monopoly, Business, Labor and Government Policies,* Baltimore: Johns Hopkins Press, 1952, pp. 389–390.

[12]*Ibid.,* p. 393.

[13]Marshall, *loc. cit.,* p. 397.

[14]John T. Dunlop and Neil W. Chamberlain, eds., *Frontiers of Collective Bargaining,* "The Function of the Strike," New York: Harper and Row, 1967, pp. 103–124.

affect the economy. The language of a distinguished labor reporter after the 1959 116-day steel strike is illustrative: "The steel companies and the United Steelworkers of America have become standard bearers in what amounts to an outbreak of class warfare—low-voltage, non-violent, but nonetheless destructive in its implications for industrial democracy and an economy calculated to serve the consuming public."[15]

(c) *Significant misallocation of resources among enterprises versus no important impact.* Charles Lindblom has stated the concerns of a group of economists in these strong terms: "This is the great labor problem of our times. Unionism is destroying the competitive price system."[16] Sometimes the argument is that labor organizations combine against the consumer and the public interest to distort wages and profits from some idealized or competitive norm, while on other occasions the mechanism is adversarial collective bargaining that increases wages and reduces employment in an enterprise or sector, thereby creating unemployment and lower wages in other sectors of the economy. In the current setting, the argument is that collective bargaining has raised compensation so high in basic steel, automobiles, rubber, and agricultural implements as to have contributed materially to the economic decline of these sectors.

The response of the defenders of organization is to recognize that the issue is substantially a factual and definitional matter. What distortions are in fact created and what structure of resources and compensation would exist without unions? Further, collective bargaining is said to take wages out of competition and compel employers to compete on the basis of managerial efficiency. At times one may recognize that an area of uniformity has been extended too far, as in rubber tire rates extended to rubber shoes or to rubber belts, in the same enterprise. However, collective bargaining is a flexible process and can correct such excesses in response to market competition.

(d) *Persistent serious inflation versus the view that unionization is not a major factor.* Some economists have accused the institutions of collective bargaining of being a major contributor to inflation. The views expressed vary from the judgment that collective bargaining imparts a small inflationary bias to wages to the more radical proposition that unions create inflation so extreme that the competitive price system will be abandoned in the search for remedies.

On the other hand, much of contemporary economics treats inflation as a far more complex matter. Monetarists emphasize the significance of increases in money supply, while other macroeconomists emphasize fiscal and exchange rate policies in their influences on prices, wages, and employment. The independent role of unionization is very difficult to ascribe.

---

[15]*Challenges to Collective Bargaining,* The American Assembly, Englewood Cliffs, New Jersey: Prentice-Hall, 1967, pp. 169–170.

[16]Charles E. Lindblom, *Unions and Capitalism,* New Haven: Yale University Press, 1949, p. 4.

Beyond these four main themes in the debate over the consequences of labor organization, it is appropriate to recognize that there may be economic consequences from government activities stimulated by unions, just as there are economic consequences in each of the four areas noted above derived from governmental activities stimulated by business interests.[17]

At least some brief comments are required on the very extensive literature, still growing very rapidly, that seeks to measure the effects of organization in the labor market. In general, these studies conclude that collective bargaining raises compensation in modest amounts, thereby reducing employment in union sectors. The effect of collective bargaining on compensation is greater in recession, by preventing wage cuts, than in prosperity when wages may lag behind price increases.

There are rather fundamental questions about the basic methodology and the data applied to the measurement of labor organization that have not often been raised:

(a) The impact of labor organization is rather poorly measured by the number of employees covered by collective agreements or by union membership. Some large companies have establishments that are organized and others that are not. The presence of partial organization is a powerful factor in company policy, influencing wages, benefits, and other personnel rules. The presence of organization in a locality, community, or sector may have similar consequences. The extent of union and nonunion wages and benefits thus may be both seriously misrepresented in conventional comparisons.

(b) There is a fundamental difference between most union and nonunion compensation arrangements that these comparisons do not well recognize. Union wage and benefit schedules are changed periodically on a group basis, although wage or salary ranges may be administered in some small degree on an individual basis. However, nonunion wages are largely adjusted on an individual basis, especially in smaller enterprises. Comparisons of average hourly earnings among union and nonunion industries are not strictly commensurate: in union enterprises average hourly earnings do not well reflect wage schedule changes, while nonunion enterprises or industries make no wage schedule changes to measure.

(c) The most significant impact of unionization, according to insightful students of industrial relations, has been on management itself. Managing without a union is quite different from managing with a union, and many times the same manager is not able to shift style from one to the other. None of this is captured by the data.

---

[17]For a general discussion of the consequences of collective bargaining, see Derek C. Bok and John T. Dunlop, *Labor and the American Community,* New York: Simon & Schuster, 1970, pp. 207–228.

(d) Finally, to revert to a point as old as John Stuart Mill and Alfred Marshall, there are many considerations other than the effects of unions on the national product. "Except on matters of mere detail, there are perhaps no practical questions even among those which approach nearest to the character of pure economic questions which admit of being decided on economic premises alone."[18] Much more is at stake at the workplace than economics: fairness, equity among workers, industrial democracy, safety and health, and other values of society.

My own conclusion from all these arguments regarding the consequences of labor organization is rather simple. The issue is not one of logic but of actual experience. There are, no doubt, some collective bargaining relationships that restrain productivity, distort wages and prices, are full of bitter conflict, and contribute to inflation, just as there are numerous other collective bargaining relationships that have more positive effects upon the national product and the larger society. The econometric work has hardly helped in a practical sense to distinguish among relationships and to develop approaches that may be ameliorative.

VITALIZATION IN U.S. MARKET COMPETITION

These days the U.S. is full of analyses, prescriptions, and programs from economists, politicians, editorial writers, and even soothsayers to vitalize the U.S. economy. For some, the program is liberation of the U.S. economy from taxation and government regulations. For others, it is more government support for research and development and more basic science education. For Robert B. Reich, the old ways of "high volume and standardization" and "paper entrepreneurialism" are the source of the problem, to be replaced by "flexible-system production characterized by technological innovation, precision manufacturing and customization of products."[19]

For still others, the steel and automobile industries' presumed alliance between labor and business, with increasing quest for tariff protection and quotas on imports, is the problem. There are those who advocate the Japanese model of management and labor relations, whatever that may mean. Others place the blame on big business, contending the strategy of maximizing the wealth of stockholders or the rate of return on investment is too short term in its outlook. "The key to long-term success—even survival—in business is what it has always been: to invest, to innovate, to lead, to create value where none existed

---

[18]Marshall, *loc. cit.*, p. 410.

[19]Robert B. Reich, "The Next American Frontier," *The Atlantic*, Volume 251, No. 3, April 1983, pp. 43–58.

before. Such determination, such striving to excel, requires leaders—not *just* controllers, market analysts, and portfolio managers."[20]

Others argue that the external oil price shocks and the prolonged recession have materially aggravated ordinary problems of transition. The structural change whereby a much larger proportion of U.S. enterprises has become subject to international competition is no doubt a major long-term development.

My experience and analyses of industrial relations systems lead to the view that basic features of labor and management are not readily transferred from one advanced country to another. I do not believe that we can or are likely to import Japanese labor–management arrangements any more than General MacArthur was able to impose the Taft–Hartley law in an earlier era on Japan. That is not to say that we may not adapt to our diverse arrangements some features from each other.

Another point requires recognition: while U.S. industrial relations have certain common features, there is vast diversity among our labor–management relationships, under collective bargaining or without unions; there is probably greater diversity in the U.S. than within the Japanese system, since the U.S. is larger and less homogeneous in many ways.

In my view, there are at least four requisites for labor organizations and collective bargaining to meet the challenges of economic vitalization and market competition in the U.S. in the years ahead:

(a) There must be a significant transformation in the skills and training of the labor force to meet the rigors of competition, new markets, and the drastic changes arising in a labor force with more women, minorities, a different age distribution, more education, new occupations, and new regional locations. Training and retraining needs to be shared between the public and private sectors, but there is a significant role for collective bargaining as in the recent collective bargaining argument between the United Automobile Workers and the Ford Motor Company.

(b) The permanently high degree of interdependence of the U.S. economy with the world economy requires that wage- and benefit-setting processes are regularly more responsive and responsible to international competition. While many other factors intervene, such as tariff and nontariff trade regulations and exchange rate fluctuations, the reference to international competition is a new orientation for many collective bargaining and labor–management relations.

(c) The period ahead will demand more concern with the means to increase total productivity. In some relationships this may be achieved in more cooper-

---

[20]Robert H. Hayes and William J. Abernathy, "Managing Our Way to Economic Decline," *Harvard Business Review*, July–August, 1980, Vol. 58, No. 4, p. 77.

ative and participatory ways, while in others it may be achieved with considerable conflict and the stern exercise of management initiatives that reflect the absence of consent or agreement. There is likely to be no single pattern of labor–management relations to enhance productivity.[21]

(d) There is a desperate necessity in the U.S. for business, labor, and government to demonstrate a new willingness to have systematic dialogue over common problems and to establish a forum for this purpose at both national and state levels. The present and past patterns of ideological conflict and excessive legalisms have prevented reasonable cooperative activity, save in wartime. Problem solving and political compromise are requisite to economic vitalization.[22]

[21]D. Q. Mills, "Reforming the U.S. System of Collective Bargaining," *Monthly Labor Review*, Vol. 106, No. 3, March 1983, pp. 18–22.

[22]John T. Dunlop, "Growth, Unemployment and Inflation," in International Chamber of Commerce, *Economic Growth*, 26th Congress, *Enterprise, Freedom and the Future*, Paris, 1978.

Information Disclosure in the Corporation

B. C. ROBERTS

Professor of Industrial Relations
The London School of Economics and Political Science
England

Information is a fundamental ingredient of all rational decisions. Without accurate, relevant, understandable, and timely information, decisions must be made on the basis of assumptions, rumors, suspicions, hopes, and fears. Even though we are in a period when the flow of information has become a deluge, when news is immediately available and events occurring anywhere in the world can be seen in our living rooms, and when facts and figures on virtually every subject can be retrieved and displayed at the push of a button, there is nevertheless considerable controversy over the extent to which employers should be compelled to disclose information to their employees.

Presumably, the idea that information ought to be as freely available as possible would be widely accepted in a democratic society. Information is not, however, a neutral factor; it may benefit one person or many people at the expense of others. Access to information is seen by both management and unions as a factor that is of crucial importance to their relative power and ability to achieve their respective goals. Information could thus provoke conflict as well as help to resolve it. The significance of information frequently depends on how it is selected and disseminated, and how it is received and acted upon. Nor is information a cost-free product: it has to be produced and disseminated, and this may be expensive. Who should produce the information essential to good industrial relations and who should bear this cost? The extent to which the flow of information could be improved and the impact that this might have on industrial relations requires careful examination.

THE STATE PROVISION OF GENERAL INFORMATION

More than a century ago, the governments of the U.S., Great Britain, and Germany began to collect and publish at regular intervals data concerning the labor market. Other industrialized countries soon followed. Statistical information on many aspects of wages, prices, productivity, the labor force, strikes, trade union membership, and a variety of other matters is of vital importance to policy making at all levels. It enables comparisons to be made by the parties involved in an industrial relations system and it has a significant effect on their actions. Traditional data of this kind are frequently disaggregated on the basis of standardized occupational, industrial, and geographical categories, but this normally often stops short of classifications that would allow particular enterprises to be identified. Anonymity is a basic principle of the supply and publication of this type of data.

The limitations of such data are recognized and they are now frequently supplemented by special studies commissioned by government departments and by research carried out in universities and by private organizations. Such studies are often used as a foundation for policy changes and legislative action. Governments, employers, and unions are not always willing cooperators because these studies may have implications that affect their activities. Each party inevitably welcomes or challenges findings that it believes support or damage its interests. Nonetheless, it is the duty of governments to ensure a continuous flow of statistical information and to promote vigorous research programs in the public interest.

THE DISCLOSURE OF INFORMATION BY EMPLOYERS

The amount of information provided voluntarily by management on all aspects of business activity has considerably increased under social pressures generated by trends toward more open, less inhibited and restrictive societies. The most successful companies in Europe, North America, and Japan have been pioneers of this development.

In principle, it can be argued that whoever is going to be significantly affected by a decision has a right to be informed in advance of all the relevant facts and to have an opportunity to influence the decision. This argument may present management with a number of difficulties:

(1) It can make the decision more difficult to make and costly to carry out if it is opposed in advance.

(2) It may weaken the authority of management and increase union bargaining power.

(3) Since information is often costly to collect and disseminate, it makes decision-making more expensive.

(4) It may stir up conflict unnecessarily, with adverse effects on industrial relations.

(5) It may lead to a leakage of confidential information that might benefit competitors.

These fears may be exaggerated but they are not unreal. Information sharing does have an impact on the balance of bargaining power. Since managers are charged with the responsibility of initiating, planning, and executing decisions and are held accountable if they are not successful, they are naturally concerned that the disclosure of some information may undermine their authority and their ability to carry out their functions.

Management believes that it must have a significant element of discretion as to the substance and the timing of information that is disclosed to employees and the public. The extent to which management can rely on its employees not to abuse or exploit information will depend to a large extent on the level of trust that exists. Greater degrees of confidence reduce the probability that management's fears will be realized. Confidence and trust will not grow, however, unless management is prepared to be as open and informative as possible. If openness is recognized as the general policy of management, managers will continue to be respected when they withhold information they believe would be untimely and possibly damaging to the interests of the company.

Information is qualitatively different and relates to decisions and developments at different levels. At the company level, the information of concern to employees may relate to the overall performance of the enterprise, to major decisions relative to expansion and contraction, to the advent of new technology, new procedures, and methods of work, and to new conditions of employment. This information may be highly relevant to the employee's unions and may possibly be the subject of collective bargaining.

It is essential to good relations that the channels of communication be kept open vertically and laterally throughout the organization. Blockages at any point have effects that spread through the communications network. Only if there is a constant monitoring of information flows will it be possible to prevent random or persistent blockages from occurring and adversely affecting communications. This will require a corporate policy that is pursued vigorously and sustained by appropriate procedures.

At the departmental level, the flow of information of the greatest importance is likely to relate to factors connected with the work task. Absence of information when a production process is held up by lack of supplies or breakdowns in machinery, or when a change in working methods is made by management without prior information and consultation, is a common cause of discontent and diminishes cooperation. It is a prime task of supervision and the lower levels of management to keep employees as fully informed as possible on all issues that affect their work performance. Lower levels of management cannot do this effectively if they are not themselves effectively briefed. Joint problem-solving committees in the U.S. and quality circles in Japan are good examples of the value of information sharing. This kind of consultation is useful in finding solutions to production problems by a voluntary process, which closely involves workers and managers at the departmental level. It must be noted that the success of quality circles owes a great deal to the strong bonds of cooperation that reinforce relations between workers and managers in the Japanese system of industrial relations. In the context of adversarial industrial relations and under the stresses generated by recession in Western countries, joint problem-solving committees have encountered considerable problems of survival.

LEGAL REQUIREMENTS ON THE DISCLOSURE OF INFORMATION

In most Western European countries there has been, since the 1950s, a body of legislation that imposes an obligation on employers to provide works councils or trade union representatives with information relating to employment security, job evaluation, pay rates and structures, and prospective changes in conditions of employment and methods of work.

However, companies have to be careful in supplying more information to their employees than to shareholders, since this might be in conflict with the interests of those who hold the company's stock. Many companies have begun to extend their annual reports by presenting a supplementary report of an explanatory nature to their employees. Under an amendment to the 1982 Employment Act in the U.K., it will be necessary in the future for companies to report annually on the action company directors have taken to provide employees systematically through their managers or supervisors with information on matters of concern to them as employees. They will also be called upon to report the extent to which they have consulted employees or their representatives on a regular basis before decisions were made that would be likely to affect their interests. Further, they must state the steps they have taken to achieve a common awareness on the part of managers and employees on the problems involved in allocating resources for such purposes as pay and investment.

Disclosure of information is closely linked with consultation and collective bargaining in most European countries. Since under West German law, works councils have a right of veto or delay over proposed changes in certain employment practices, such as job evaluation or dismissal, they must be given prior information.

Belgium has perhaps the most comprehensive legal requirements on the disclosure of information among the EEC countries. Information must be provided by employers to the works council on a wide range of basic employment, financial, and organizational facts as they relate to the current and future activities of the enterprise. This information must be provided in writing annually and orally (with written summaries where necessary) every three months, and whenever events occur that can have important repercussions on the undertaking and its employees. In every case where a management decision may have such an impact, for example, collective layoffs or work reorganization, the information must be provided in advance of the decision and for consultation to take place.

In the U.S. and the U.K. disclosure of information required by law has been specifically related to collective bargaining. Under the concept of the obligation to bargain in "good faith" laid down by the National Labor Relations Act, there is an implicit requirement in the U.S. that employers must supply such information as the unions need in order to bargain effectively. If information is not considered to be "presumptively relevant," the union must show need. Where an employer argues inability to meet a pay claim, he must be prepared to open his books to the union to establish the validity of his rejection of the union's demands.

In the U.K. there is no requirement to disclose any specific items of information, but under the 1975 Employment Protection Act employers are placed under a general duty to disclose to representatives of trade unions information that is

(1) necessary for collective bargaining purposes,
(2) would be in accordance with good industrial relations to disclose.

An employer is not compelled to disclose information if it

(1) is against the interests of national security,
(2) is against the law,
(3) relates to an individual,
(4) has been disclosed to the employer in confidence,
(5) is the subject of legal proceedings,
(6) would cause substantial injury to the employer for reasons other than collective bargaining.

The general duty of an employer to disclose information is limited to disclosure to a shop steward or union official and not to employees in general. It is also limited to information without which trade union representatives would be materially impeded in carrying out collective bargaining in accordance with good industrial relations practice.

The aim of the Employment Protection Act is to balance the legitimate need of the trade union to have access to information it requires for effective collective bargaining and the need of the employer not to disclose information that the interests of the business would deem to be confidential. Nor is an employer required to disclose information that would not normally be available without engaging in research and analysis. Since an employer is under no obligation to disclose information he believes would be damaging to the interests of the enterprise, the Employment Protection Act imposes no limitation on the freedom of the union to keep confidential any information its members or their representatives receive. In the other countries in Western Europe where similar disclosure provisions exist, union representatives are under an obligation not to pass on information to their members when it has been disclosed under a seal of confidentiality.

It is difficult to measure the effect of laws providing for the compulsory disclosure of information in relation to collective bargaining. There is evidence that companies with well-developed systems of collective bargaining and joint consultation have become more informative without the unions having to make use of the law. This may have been due to economic circumstances during the past few years when employers have been anxious to prove to the unions they could not afford the improvements in pay and conditions sought by the unions. In this context, unions have had little incentive to seek information that in all probability would have confirmed the employer's case. Not all union leaders believe more information necessarily strengthens their bargaining position. They feel less inhibited in bringing pressure to bear on employers when they are not fully informed as to the employer's economic situation. There is no evidence to suggest that the greater availability of information has had a material effect on industrial relations in general or on the specific field of union action such as the decision to strike. Information may have an important influence on decisions of this kind, but which kind of information and how it actually influences attitudes and behavior has not been effectively researched.

DISCLOSURE OF INFORMATION RELATING TO REDUCTIONS IN EMPLOYMENT

One area that has given rise to much employee concern and is covered by legal rights in most Western European countries is the issue of reductions in employment due to plant closures and the introduction of new technology. Throughout Western Europe companies intending to reduce the size of their work force by dismissals must inform in advance not only their employees' works council and trade union representatives but also government employment agencies.

Vigorous collective bargaining is common with regard to the numbers and categories of employees to be laid off and the financial compensation to which they will be entitled. In most countries the law lays down the minimum conditions an employer must observe, and these are often improved upon. In Italy, for example, employers must maintain an employees' indemnity fund, which will provide an eligible employee with a full year's wage or salary for whatever reason he is compelled to leave his employment.

The issue of information relative to closure has been a matter of bitter controversy between the National Coal Board and the National Union of Mineworkers in the U.K. during the past few years. The mineworkers' union has claimed that the National Coal Board has a secret list of coal mines it wishes to close down for economic reasons. The board has refused to confirm or deny that it would like to close down all its uneconomic mines, but it is doubtful if it can continue losing hundreds of millions of pounds on these mines. The issue is not the facts relating to these uneconomic mines but the determination of the union to resist closure on any terms and the objective of the board to reduce its economic loss without a damaging conflict with the union. If the board were to identify the sites in question, the unions would be able to unify their employees in opposition and a massive confrontation would probably be unavoidable. In the long run, however, the closure of these mines probably is inevitable since most of them are running out of coal.

The requirement to disclose information on prospective plant closures and redundancies has neither eliminated large-scale layoffs, nor conflicts over them but such layoffs now require a reasonable period of notice and appropriate compensation.

THE VREDELING DIRECTIVE

In 1980 the European Commission put forward a draft directive that, if approved, is binding on all member states of the EEC relating to the disclosure of information in multinational enterprises with subsidiaries in the EEC whether or not the parent company is located in the EEC. The directive states that the management of a dominant undertaking (i.e., a parent company), if it is located in a member state, should be required to disclose at least every six months, via the management of its subsidiaries, information to employees' representatives in all subsidiaries employing at least 100 employees in the EEC.

This information should relate to

(a) structure and manning,

(b) the economic and financial situation,

(c) the situation and probable development of the business and of production and sales,

(d) the employment situation and probable trends,

(e) production and investment programs,

(f) rationalization plans,

(g) manufacturing and working methods, in particular, the introduction of new working methods,

(h) all procedures and places liable to have a substantial effect on employees' interests.

Where the management of a dominant undertaking proposes to make a decision concerning the whole or a major part of the undertaking or one of its subsidiaries relating to the closure or transfer of an establishment or a major part, restrictions, extensions, or substantial modifications to the activities of the undertaking, major organizational modifications, or the introduction of long-term cooperation with other undertakings or the cessation of such cooperation, then the following applies:

- The information must be given to representatives of the employees, who have 30 days in which to convey the views of their constituents to management.
- If a body representing employees already exists at a level higher than an individual subsidiary, the information shall be given by management to this body. If such a body does not exist, it may be created.
- If the dominant undertaking is outside the EEC and it does not designate at least one person within the EEC able to fulfill the requirements of the directive, the disclosure responsibilities will fall upon the subsidiary employing the largest number within the EEC.

Member states are called upon to introduce laws, regulations, and administrative provisions necessary to comply with the directive. These include laws to impose penalties in case employers fail to fulfill the obligations to disclose the information specified and to engage in consultation, where this is required, with the representatives of the employees. Members of bodies representing employees and authorized delegates are required to maintain discretion with regard to confidential information, and in communication with third parties they are not permitted to divulge secrets regarding the enterprises concerned. Member states are called upon to set up national bodies to settle disputes concerning confidentiality and to impose appropriate penalties in cases of infringement.

The directive has been strongly opposed by employers' organizations throughout the EEC, who believed it went too far: namely that it would be unnecessarily costly to operate, that it would undermine the authority of local management, and that it would endanger legitimate confidentiality. Several amendments have been made to diminish these adverse effects, but the proposed directive still raises some issues of concern.

Because several countries have differing procedures for consultation, a uniform system could prove troublesome to implement. However, the significance of this directive is in its attempt to impose a uniform system of information disclosure throughout the EEC.

Most unions believe that the directive, as amended, will give them little additional power over that which already exists under collective agreements and national laws, EEC and OECD guidelines, and the ILO declaration on the obligations of multinational enterprises; nevertheless, they would like to see the directive adopted.

CONCLUSIONS

It is clear from contemporary evidence that there is a growing belief, which is accepted by management, unions, and governments, that the disclosure of information has a significant role to play in the fostering of good industrial relations and improved productivity. It is also clear, however, from experience in Europe, the U.S., and Japan that the sharing of information does not provide a simple solution for problems that are deeply rooted in the cultural climate of industrial relations.

Unions inevitably see access to more information as a means of increasing their bargaining power. For this reason, employers are often skeptical of the benefits that a greater disclosure of information to trade unions would achieve. On the other hand, they have become increasingly aware that under modern conditions openness and improved communications are essential to the improvement of relations with their employees.

There is a need to satisfy the legitimate requirements and reservations of employers and employees and their unions if the broadened scope of information disclosure is to make more positive contributions. Since only managers are in a position to know whether the disclosure of particular items of information could be seriously damaging to the interests of the company, there are good practical grounds for permitting them an element of discretion with regard both to the content and timing of information given to their employees and the unions or works councils. This must not, however, be used as an excuse to deprive employees of the information that would inspire their confidence, facilitate their trust, and reduce unnecessary conflict.

A Rationale for Employment Security[1]

GLENN E. WATTS

President
Communication Workers of America
United States

EMPLOYMENT SECURITY ISSUES

Workers' concern about employment security heightened as unemployment grew dramatically during the most recent recession. In addition, two major structural changes in the world economy have intensified workers' current anxiety over employment security.

The first of these major structural changes is the development of new production technologies based on the microprocessor and robots. Major new advances in production technology based on microprocessors with large potential employment implications are now being implemented by industry. These new technologies are not limited to any specific industry—in manufacturing, we are witnessing the development of a new phenomenon. In Japan, Fujitsu Fanuc has recently built a factory that reportedly operates without workers during the evening shift. In the machine tools industry, CAD/CAM design and production is an increasingly widespread computer-based technology. In telecommunications, vast new computerized systems are changing job structure and content. And in the office, word processing and distributed data processing are changing the nature of work. From the invention of the transistor in 1956 has come the vision of the workerless factory and the computerized office. At a time of stagnant economic growth and rising unemployment, workers are anxious over the possi-

---

[1]This article was written in December, 1982. Since that time the Communications Workers of America and AT&T have completed another round of collective bargaining during which they established common-interest forums and a training and retraining fund. Overshadowing all other developments in the communications industry has been the breakup of the Bell System into seven regional operating companies and an independent AT&T. The reorganization of the industry further increases the need for greater employment security.

ble threat of dislocation by robots or new production systems. Their anxiety is magnified as the demands on them to perform their work are also changing. Work routines and skills developed over many years of employment are lost as a new generation of production systems or machines is introduced at the workplace.

These changes are accelerating rapidly and are perceived as a dual threat to the jobs of workers. First, will the number of jobs be sufficient? Have we entered a period of high structural unemployment? Second, will the skills of today's workers match those required by the new jobs? Will the content of the new jobs be satisfying? These are the challenges to employment security that technology presents to the labor movement.

As if the revolution in production methods were not enough to create anxiety over employment security, we are also in the midst of a worldwide restructuring of economic production. It is now clear that the U.S. is no longer an isolated economic entity. The multinational corporations that began transferring production facilities abroad in the 1960s evolved into worldwide integrated producers. Automobiles, textiles, and electronics are all now produced, distributed, and marketed through complex worldwide systems. In fact, this centrifugal economic dispersion demands greater inputs of information age services, data processing, and communications to bind the new world system together.

The reorganization of the structure of the world's economy has been set in motion with little regard for workers' employment security. Workers in the U.S. see thousands of jobs exported abroad or moved to the southern areas of the country. In one region, factories and schools stand idle, while in another rapid growth overwhelms the available social services. With U.S. production challenged import penetration continues to climb. This climate of dislocation, displacement, and record levels of unemployment casts a shadow of insecurity over all workers.

UNION INVOLVEMENT

American trade unions have sought to alleviate employment insecurity through collective bargaining and social and economic legislation. At the level of the firm, collective bargaining is the main tool used to enhance employee income security. Through negotiations, the Communications Workers of America (CWA) has created benefits and programs to mitigate the human impact of changes in technology and business organization, among them the following:

- Supplemental Income Protection Plan: these benefits are made available to eligible workers declared surplus by the company because of technology, to a maximum of $18,000 per year.

• Technological Displacement: this gave workers the alternative to accept a termination allowance instead of being transferred to a lower-rated position because of technological change.
• Reassignment Pay Protection Plan: this ensures that long-term employees who are downgraded because of technological change will suffer no reduction in pay.

While these contractual protections cushion the impact of dislocation from technological change or business reorganization, they are not sufficient to ensure employment security in the new economic environment. All our members share the same primary concern—the potential threat to employment security from technological change, but traditionally employment security in the face of technological change has not been a high priority of the U.S. labor movement. In certain industries in specific time periods, it has been important, but within the context of a growing economy, labor as a whole has sought to increase its overall share of the economic pie rather than protect any one part of it.

This philosophy is best characterized by a statement attributed to John L. Lewis, the fiery leader of the United Mine Workers of America: "I don't care about what technology coal operators use or how many miners are required, just so long as they are the best paid workers in America."

Dealing directly with the employment security problem raised by technology is difficult because it runs against the historic bargain struck by labor with management as articulated by Lewis. In this accord, labor accepted management's claim to determine production technology and employment levels, in return for which workers would receive higher pay. In its time, this approach served an important purpose by raising real wages, but it has also created a framework and history that make it difficult to confront the direct impact of technology on workers and to increase their employment security.

Labor realizes this bargain is no longer sufficient or satisfactory. There is a widespread perception of membership dissatisfaction with work, and change must occur. This is why the CWA sanctioned a "job pressures" day in 1979 and has moved in nontraditional ways to increase employment security.

Technology has been transforming the telephone industry at such an extraordinary pace that our members must insist on new job protections. Nine years ago all telephone central offices were based on electromechanical switches. Today, more than one half of them are computer-controlled electronic switching systems. The new systems have been introduced in a manner that increases the pace of work and renders traditional contract provisions obsolete.

Technology intrinsically changes all it touches. Our commitment to protecting the rights of workers has not changed, but the new technology has given management a level of control over workers that would never have been secured at the bargaining table. By developing new systems that inevitably fracture jobs, deskill organized workers, and increase individual monitoring and record keeping, the new technology can be used as a weapon against the work force and the unions that represent them.

The computers and the microelectronic components that make the emerging systems possible are neither pro- nor antiworker but will do the bidding of whoever develops the systems. If labor is to succeed in creating employment security in the face of rapidly changing technology and resulting managerial control, we must do more than set limits on them after they are developed and on line. We must establish a continuous dialogue in shaping the changes. If we hope to provide the membership with the same level of control and protection as we have in the past, we must press forward along these nontraditional paths to give employment security to those we represent. This logic has led to our joint cooperative ventures, and it should eventually lead to union participation in the conception, design, testing, and implementation of new technology. This is the only way to ensure that workers are the beneficiaries and not the victims of new technological systems.

After analyzing past successes and failures, we decided it was necessary to reformulate our traditional, adversarial relationship with management. On the whole, the role of U.S. labor unions has been confined to a reactive posture by limiting or opposing changes proposed by management. These limits were self-imposed. As Samuel Gompers, a founder of the American Labor Movement, said some 60 years ago: "Collective bargaining proposes that employees shall have the right to organize and to deal with employers through selected representatives as to wages and working conditions. There is no belief held that its members shall control the plants or usurp the rights of owners."[2]

At the CWA, which represents 650,000 information industry workers, we are starting to explore ways to move beyond the limits set by Gompers and to form new relationships with management. We took our first steps in this new direction to achieve employment security in 1980 during an important round of negotiations with AT&T, where CWA represents more than half a million workers. In these negotiations, CWA and AT&T agreed to establish three joint labor–management committees: the Technology Change Committee, the Occupational Job Evaluation Committee, and the Working Conditions and Service Quality Improvement Committee.

Each of these committees signaled a willingness by labor and management to work together in a different way: this new relationship opens the door to new opportunities to improve employment security. The three programs were designed as a comprehensive attempt to deal with the issues of employment security raised by the new technology.

---

[2]Samuel Gompers, *Labor and the Employer*, New York: Dutton, 1920, p. 286.

The Technology Change Committee guarantees the union six months advance notice of any major technological changes that may affect represented employees. This includes changes in equipment, organization, or methods of operation. With this agreement, we have set a standard for the rest of the U.S. labor movement. The advance notice allows the union to anticipate the changes and to apply the various force adjustment contract clauses for affected personnel.

The other two committees help employees reap some of the benefits of technology and protect them against its adverse impacts. The mission of the Occupational Job Evaluation Committee is to develop a mutually acceptable system of ranking thousands of jobs. The union agreed to participate in the committee to ensure that workers are fairly compensated for their efforts in the changing nature of work and to encourage the maintenance of skill levels and responsibilities— two goals of our program for employment security.

The third committee, the Working Conditions and Service Quality Improvement Committee, oversees the Quality of Work Life (QWL) process, which is being implemented throughout AT&T. The QWL program was our response to the job stress created by new technologies and basically involves participation in decision-making from the lowest organizational level. There are already about 700 participation teams in operation, and joint training for labor and management is spreading the process further.

Our experience with these three joint committees has laid the foundation for further exploration to preserve employment security. The success of these experiments has whetted our appetites for further joint, cooperative ventures. Based on our own experience and that of other unions, we shall continue to propose new measures to enhance employment security.

The CWA has not been alone in seeking greater employment security through changes in management style and altering the traditional bargaining relationship. The United Auto Workers (UAW) also has been particularly active. In negotiations with General Motors and Ford, the UAW won agreement from the companies to establish two joint National Development and Training Centers with at least seven staff members from each party to determine the training needs of present and displaced workers. The programs use both internal and external sources to assist workers displaced or otherwise affected by new technology, production changes, or market adjustments. Active employees, skilled and semiskilled, can maintain and update their present job skills at the centers.

The auto industry and its major union also established Mutual Growth Forums to discuss business and governmental developments affecting the companies and the union. The forums will meet quarterly at the plant level and the union's representative may address the corporate board of directors twice a year. The UAW made other substantial strides toward employment security. Generally, management argues that its decision to close a plant is solely its decision.

Nonetheless, during bargaining, the UAW reversed the company's decision to close four plants.

In addition to the joint training program, the UAW bargained for a new tuition refund program for laid-off workers. The tuition reimbursement for training at accredited institutions will aid the retraining of displaced workers. Two pilot projects to enhance employment security were also negotiated: At six plants, the UAW won lifetime employment guarantees for 80% of the workers at the pilot plants. A second approach guarantees workers' income without guaranteeing employment. In this pilot program, called Guaranteed Income Stream, employees with 15 years of service are guaranteed 50% of their hourly rate until they reach 62 or retire, whichever comes first. Disability, health, and life insurance benefits will be provided for employees in this program. In case of permanent layoff due to a plant closing, the threshold for eligibility decreases to ten years of service. In both cases, additional years of service increase the guaranteed income stream up to 75% of prelayoff earnings. Workers must also remain registered with the company and the state employment office and accept alternative employment arranged by the company.

In the electrical industry, the unions representing workers at General Electric and Westinghouse also improved their contracts with regard to employment security. Job security has grown into an increasingly important issue for the electrical unions as the industry has resorted to exporting work abroad, subcontracting, increased use of robots, and automation. These gains include: new pay protections for workers who are displaced, transferred, or laid off because of automation, work transfer, or plant shutdowns; advance notice of six months for plant closings or work transfers and 60 days for the installation of robots or automation of production work; new programs to help employees find jobs and learn new skills, including an education or retraining reimbursement of up to $1800.

JOB TRAINING

Historically, the telephone industry has had an excellent record in providing training for its work force. However, with the introduction of computer systems, automated test desks, and decreased job site control, the value of the training received in the past has been reduced. Most employees are now provided instruction in only one or two tasks and are not taught how the entire system works or their role in that system. When their jobs are eliminated because of software changes or the introduction of new hardware, they are then provided with additional task-specific training for another job that will eventually be abolished. Without a complete understanding of how the new systems work, the employees become more and more isolated from the goals of the organization, resulting in worker inefficiencies (and lost productivity). This in turn prompts management to introduce further labor-saving devices to address the labor inefficiencies that it has created.

In order to break this spiral, we must negotiate a structure that will give the union a voice in all training provided the membership. During their first year of employment, all employees should receive one full day of system training. This training should provide all employees with a thorough knowledge of how their jobs fit into the overall business structure. The training should also include an explanation of how the work is organized; the current generation of equipment; the trends in future systems and their impact on the work force; and a general timetable of when these changes will occur.

A significant reorganization of work has accompanied the introduction of new technology. A smaller and smaller range of tasks is now performed by the individual employee. Studies have shown that workers who have their jobs fractured in this manner report significantly higher stress symptoms and more alienation from work than those whose jobs are more varied. This obviously leads to lower productivity. Simpler jobs are also more adaptable to automation. In order to encourage the development of human-centered, productive technology, the CWA will ask for job rotation so that all employees perform all the tasks within their job titles on a regular and equal basis.

Broadening the job content for workers is an important new direction for increased job security and productivity. For example, one proposal we have considered is staffing ''traffic sensitive'' operator or directory assistance jobs at peak levels, and then assigning those personnel to other work during nonpeak hours. This would broaden the job content for these employees as well as alleviate scheduling problems. It would also require major structural changes in the physical layout of work and the compensation system. However, it is indicative of the innovative direction in which we must move.

Among our key proposals shall be a jointly administered Employee Career Development & Training Program funded by the employers. This fund would be established to accomplish four key goals:

- The program should improve the employment security, career mobility, and personal development of existing employees. This would include a requirement to give computer literacy instruction for all employees to work effectively in the information age.
- The program must provide career counseling, training and retraining, and developmental opportunities to enhance the members' job skills, abilities, and dignity.
- It must arrange or provide for training, retraining, and career development assistance for persons about to be laid off or displaced by new company arrangements, by new technologies, by shifts in competitive position, by down-sizing or closing of facilities, or by economic downturns.

- It should provide training for those involved in activities related to quality of work life, technology change, occupational job evaluation, and other efforts. The Company would benefit by having a work force better equipped to deal with changes in technology thereby improving its competitive position.

COMMUNICATION AND EMPLOYEE–MANAGEMENT RELATIONS

To participate effectively in decisions about production technology, we need to increase the length of notice and the amount of information provided to the union about the new systems. Our current pattern setting agreement on pre-notification must be expanded. Changes in computer hardware and software are the result of years of research planning, and development. To make an impact on the kinds of equipment that will flow into the work place, we must be involved from the earliest stages of development.

Positive change is possible only when progressive, cooperative attitudes exist at all levels within the companies with which the CWA is involved, but positive attitudes alone are insufficient. A mechanism for meeting regularly is needed to explore means to sustain company growth and the career development of CWA members. To provide a new approach to cooperative support for both the company and the union, the CWA will seek to establish, with each major employer, common interest forums at local and national levels as a visible adjunct to the collective bargaining process and as a complement to other joint efforts. As we envision them now, these forums would have three principal objectives:

- providing a framework to promote improved union/management relations through better communications, systematic fact-finding, and advance discussion of major business developments;
- providing a mechanism for constructive and cooperative problem solving; and,
- developing innovative human resources management and development approaches through pilot projects and experiments to enhance competitiveness and employment security.

For example, we foresee that the common interest forums would allow us to address management's use of computer-controlled equipment to monitor the work of individual employees. There is nothing inherent in the new systems that requires such record-keeping. Rather, management is using the new technology to increase its control and to establish and maintain conditions of employment without bargaining over them. Such record-keeping is strictly prohibited in Sweden and should be prohibited in the U.S. as well. The capability of easily monitoring specific tasks encourages the development of such tasks when work is being reorganized. Furthermore, these indexes or criteria, while readily measurable, often provide false benchmarks for managers and workers. Making the index becomes the goal, while providing the real product or service suffers. By prohibiting the use of computers to monitor individual work performance, we shall be relieving workers of a significant stress factor and encouraging management not to organize work around their increased ability to monitor.

Fundamentally, what these bargaining proposals are trying to change is "management style." By this, we mean the set of attitudes and beliefs—especially about people and their relationships to each other, and the set of visible mechanisms based on those beliefs—upon which management of the organization is judged.

The "classic" attitude of managers toward workers stems from the labor conflicts of the early industrial period. The suspicion and mistrust generated at that time led to a "tough" position by managers, i.e., that bosses must hold a monopoly on power and workers should do what they are told. Participation and cooperation were impossible. Power came from position in a hierarchy rather than from shared knowledge. Frederick Taylor's "scientific management" perfected a system of tight control.

There are probably few managers today who believe totally in this hard line. There has always been some tendency toward a very different set of beliefs, one based on *human* values. Managers know that workers are motivated by a desire to give good service and to develop their capacities as well as by material wants. Good leaders have emerged who see their role as providing resources for their subordinates rather than giving orders. They have tried to establish a climate of trust and reciprocity in their organizations.

Union members contend, however, that these cooperative attitudes are being lost as rapidly as the technology is changing. This view has led the company and our union to develop the QWL process, which must be extended to restore productivity and employment security. Survey data show that dissatisfaction in many cases is as strong among managers as among workers; and their unease is growing. Managers themselves feel the pressure of constant measurement and competitive relationships and have, in many cases, begun asking when *they* would get QWL.

Several elements interact to hamper the desired changes in management style:

Management Appraisal: Managers are rewarded not for developing their employees but for producing short-term and bottom-line results. An investment in improved relationships, which is likely to pay off only in the longer run, is penalized by the existing appraisal system.

Measurements: "The numbers" are one of the most important elements in rewards for managers. Because numbers are so emphasized, qualitative measures lose out.

This problem is difficult to resolve because many results are not easily quantifiable. The spirit of teamwork and cooperation generated by participation may show up only at moments of significant change or crisis. And, no numbers can capture the sense of self-worth that results from being treated with dignity.

Also, there are things which should be measured and are not. Rarely, when "productivity" is discussed, is the ratio of management to workers factored in, but that is a major cost. "If we continue to opt for more and tighter employee controls," concludes one corporate report on the topic, "we should reach a point where our customers simply can't afford to pay for them." Another study estimated the "costs of mistrust," excessive supervision and "checking," to be 50% of the total payroll. Since QWL can lead to increased span of control, it can

TABLE I
Differences between Traditional Management Style and QWL Management Style

	Traditional Style	QWL Style
Attitudes		
Leadership	Control	Participation
	Management is boss	Management is resource
	Monopolize power; power is positional	Leadership based on knowledge, not position
Motivation	Primarily economic	Economic, social, and human development
	Mistrust	Trust based on reciprocity
Relationships	Competitive among managers; adversarial with union	Development of cooperation
Mechanisms		
Management appraisals	Short-term	Longer-term
	Bottom-line	Encourage teamwork and participation
Measurements	Quantitative	Quantitative and qualitative
Planning	Centralized; top down	Both centralized goals and decentralized participation
	One best way	Different approaches
Technology	Centralizing	Decentralized
	Deskilling	Maintains skills
	Increased control	Control at work site
Training	Narrow	Broad training in problem-solving and systems understanding
Work structures (job design)	Fragmented jobs	Autonomy, significance, wholeness, and variety
	Uniformity	Teamwork
Work rules	Centrally determined; detailed and rigid	Determined with involvement

make the organization more efficient in ways which are not captured in present "numbers." At the shopfloor level, QWL has already led to relaxation of the measurement pressure in some areas which are indicators of changes that could be made in measurement systems throughout the organization.

Planning: People at all levels of the system complain that changes are introduced with insufficient communication and preparation. One result is a sense of insecurity. Another is poor performance: we have observed many cases of changes that were unnecessarily slow and disruptive because the people involved did not understand what was happening, much less get a chance to contribute ideas.

However, many companies have involved unions and employees in planning for change. Such involvement is a central and successful feature of the Japanese management system and has been used widely in plant design and engineering in the auto industry. Consistently, the results have been unusually rapid and smooth transitions.

Management style is a corollary of labor and work relationships. Table I summarizes what we see as the differences between traditional and QWL management style. We have divided these into attitudes and mechanisms to show the full extent of change required.

INDUSTRIAL POLICY

While labor has made significant gains through collective bargaining, employment security cannot be realized unless economic and industrial policy are developed to sustain it. To create an economic framework more conducive to providing employment security, we are pursuing a rational public industrial policy for the U.S. The U.S. cannot afford to let its industrial base atrophy further nor waste its most valuable asset, human capital.

Government's traditional economic tools—monetary and fiscal policy—must be supplemented by sectoral and regional industrial policies. While there has been widespread recognition of the need for an industrial policy, there is no consensus about what its goals and program should be. An effective industrial policy should be guided by labor's historic values: full employment, income security and equity, and nondiscrimination so that all may benefit. Some of the new values discussed here could also be incorporated appropriately into such a policy, including greater worker participation and training programs. Industrial policy should go beyond creating full employment in the quantitative sense. It should also ensure the quality of those jobs and opportunities for workers to increase productivity by realizing the full potential of their creativity.

Increased productivity is seen by many as the way to break the grip of stagnation on the world economy. Worldwide reorganization of production and technology is revaluing existing capital plant. There is a pervasive phenomenon of worldwide excess productive capacity. Increases in productivity alone will allow one firm to succeed over another, but at the same time can exacerbate the worldwide structural unemployment problems.

The human cost of reorganization has been too high and wasteful of economic as well as human resources. Managers have felt the need to raise productivity and therefore have applied the old technique of Taylorism to the new computerized technology. This has fractured jobs and tended to redistribute skills among workers more unevenly than before. In the long run, this is a costly way of doing business. It alienates workers and isolates them from the goals and values of the firm. A short-term gain may be realized, but the firm's most important asset—its employees—rapidly depreciated.

A growing body of experience suggests that productivity will be increased and society better served by integrating skills within workers rather than further segregating them. Yet it cannot take place without guaranteeing security for employees. A commitment to employment security realigns the priorities of the firm. It demands that the firm broadly train and support its employees. When treated with respect, employees will respond with renewed effort. In short, employment security is the key to unlock the vast store of productive creativity now lying dormant in workers.

These directions in job security are unlike previous efforts of workers in the U.S. We must participate more in corporate decision-making if we hope to receive an equitable share of the gains that the new technologies offer. Learning from the Japanese model, we are pursuing a course of shopfloor involvement, which will result in greater productivity and an improved quality in the goods and services produced. Learning from the European models, we are firmly convinced that continued training and retraining must be the cornerstone of any successful labor policy in the face of rapid economic and technical change. Finally, learning from our predecessors in the U.S. labor movement, we know that any gains in workers' rights require strong contract language coupled with diligent enforcement and supported by an active legislative policy. What is evolving then is a U.S. model to meet the challenges of the great period of change which lies ahead.

Employee–Management Relations in a Highly Unionized Environment

B. SVEDBERG

President and Chief Executive Officer
Ericsson Telephone (L.M.)
Sweden

THE ECONOMIC ENVIRONMENT IN SWEDEN

Sweden is rather inconveniently located in a remote northern sector of the globe. It covers an area slightly larger than Japan, but its population is much smaller, situated primarily in the southern part of the country.

Sweden is highly industrialized. Nearly one third of its work force is employed within industry, while only 5.6% is required in our highly rationalized agricultural sector. Because of our limited domestic market, industry is export oriented. Exports constitute 25% of our GNP and are of vital importance to the well-being of every Swede.

The public sector in Sweden has grown rapidly. It is estimated that expenditures in this sector in 1982 were equal to nearly 60% of our GNP, an extremely high level. The union organizations are very strong, representing—on average—four out of every five employees.

Within this environment, Ericsson—one of the world's leading manufacturers of telecommunications equipment, including office automation systems—is a typical export-oriented Swedish manufacturer. While domestic production is substantial, the home market accounts for only about 20% of sales. To survive, it has had to compete throughout the world with the other major international companies in the field and with many regional and local competitors. Approximately 32,000 out of a total of around 66,000 Ericsson Group employees were located outside Sweden at the end of 1982.

Sweden became known during the 1950s for its stable and productive labor conditions, and for the ability of management and labor to reach mutually beneficial solutions to problems. The so-called Swedish model was based on joint assumption of responsibility and on strong organizations in the labor market. These organizations had clearly defined common interests in creating competitive industries that function effectively in an international free-trading system. This harmony was not entirely self-generated. It developed against the background of an expanding world economy, which offered exceptional marketing opportunities to Swedish industry at that time. Labor, in particular, had much to gain in terms of more jobs and higher pay.

The Swedish model was characterized by these elements, among others:

- a free market economy in which 90% of industry and commerce was privately owned,
- independent and freely competitive companies,
- a labor market that was well organized and independent of the government,
- a common attitude of responsibility to society,
- peaceful solutions to problems, designed to avoid the necessity for intervention by the government,
- management–employee consultation,
- gradual improvements in the conditions of employment, and reasonable compromises when problems arose.

The rapid industrial and economic expansion that began in the 1950s in Sweden naturally required many changes and shifts in manufacturing procedures. Labor participated constructively in bringing about these changes, and the combination of innovative management, new technologies, new machinery, and other rationalization measures gave Swedish workers one of the highest living standards in the world. The new prosperity also supported a strong expansion of the public sector, notably in the area of social welfare. And the politicians—through laws, regulations, and tax policies—began to play an increasingly important role in matters which the partners in the labor market had formerly negotiated through agreements.

THE GROWTH OF REGULATION

By the 1970s, as a result of the increasing political influence of the unions, management–labor relations were dominated by a great many laws that directly affected corporate operations and productivity. For example:

- The law on security of employment: This sharply limited a company's ability to dismiss employees and required that notice be given far in advance when employees had to be released because there was no work for them.
- Laws governing holidays and other authorized absences: Swedish employees were guaranteed a minimum of five weeks vacation and the right to long leaves of absence in connection with childbirth, study programs, and other activities.
- Laws governing the activities of union representatives: These gave union

officials the right to pursue union business on company time to the degree they themselves considered appropriate.

- The law on employee representation on the boards of directors: Employees were given the right to appoint two members and two deputy members to the boards of all but a few small companies.
- The act on "codetermination in the workplace": This has had a severe impact on company operations. Among other things, it required that management inform the unions, and negotiate with them, prior to any significant change affecting the company in general, or an individual employee.
- If management and the unions cannot agree on a proposed change, the matter has to be negotiated at a higher level, which can cause serious problems when rapid decisions are necessary.
- In some cases the unions' interpretation of the law takes precedence and has to be applied; in other cases—for example, in the hiring of personnel—the union has a veto right. A union veto can be set aside only through central negotiations or through recourse to the labor court. Both steps can be time-consuming processes.

The traditional cooperation in the workplace, which was based on close cooperation between managers and employees, became formalized and rigid as a result of these conditions. Even with relatively minor questions that arise daily, the forms and regulations for informing the unions and negotiating with them had to be observed. The result has been the creation of barriers between management and the employees themselves, and the establishment by union representatives of parallel hierarchies within companies. It can now take a long time to obtain agreement on changes, and it is sometimes difficult to carry out essential decisions that should be implemented quickly. The negative impact of excessive intervention and regulation does not create an ideal environment for good working conditions or for maximizing productivity.

The Swedish economy is an integral part of an international system and is now in the same difficult economic situation as other industrialized countries. Our ability to lift ourselves out of this situation depends to a great degree on our capacity for flexibility and adjustment—and on our capacity to improve productivity. The extended difficult economic situation has sharpened general awareness of the challenge we face and has made it possible to make certain changes in a positive direction.

TECHNOLOGICAL CHANGE AND THE RETURN TO COOPERATION

The rapid rate of technical development, notably in the electronics field, is another driving force. This has already resulted in significant changes in the operations and working conditions of many companies, and the changes will be increasingly rapid in the future. There has been a clear shift from employment in production, as traditionally defined, to so-called white-collar work: designing, engineering, software development. This, in turn, imposes new demands for efficiency in the latter type of work and on the application of standards of productivity to at least the same degree that have long been well established in manufacturing.

To date, we have only witnessed the beginning of modern office automation, with its use of computers and computer-aided design and manufacturing (CAD/CAM) technology. What we have seen tells us that the work of office employees is changing radically. Therefore, it is important to create a work environment in which these changes and the demands for increased productivity can be accepted.

In this connection, the desire of the individual for influence over his or her own working conditions and the need to provide motivation and opportunities for growth in each job are becoming increasingly important. The basic problem of improving the quality of working life must be addressed, and that means dealing with such elements as morale and productivity.

These trends have resulted in a rebirth of the former spirit of mutual understanding and a conviction that only the partners in the labor market themselves can work out realistic and usable solutions in the light of today's realities. One consequence has been the so-called Development Agreement that has been reached, in the spirit of the earlier cooperation, among the top organizations in the Swedish labor market. This agreement specifies the common values held by management and labor and a willingness "to develop the efficiency, profitability, and competitiveness of companies, and to create the conditions for employment, job security, and growth in one's job." The primary significance of the Development Agreement is that it creates opportunities to achieve more practical and smoother forms of cooperation by replacing—in part at least—the laws and regulations referred to earlier. In their place, contracts and agreements adapted to the situation in each company are worked out.

The desire of the top organizations to achieve concrete results has been underscored by the establishment of a Council for Development Matters. The council's responsibilities include the following:

- following and promoting the application of the stated objectives and the continuing development of Swedish industry,
- providing recommendations and information, and
- stimulating research, including research on working life.

Members of the council include the chairmen of the top organizations that signed the agreement.

Among the concrete measures taken to date has been the establishment of a special Program Board. The assignment is to carry out a major project for the development of Swedish industry and commerce, using new technologies, improved organizational structures, and more attractive work environments. Qualified experts are being engaged to conduct practical experiments, based on pioneering examples of well-adapted and efficient use of new technologies, with special emphasis on computers in offices and factories.

This rebirth of the former Swedish spirit of cooperation and willingness to make joint efforts would not have been possible a few years ago. There are good reasons to hope that it can re-create the conditions that once contributed to the success of Swedish industry.

EMPLOYEES, UNIONS, AND THE MANAGEMENT FUNCTION AT ERICSSON

Employees in Sweden are unionized to a higher degree than in any other free market country. Ninety percent of our factory workers are affiliated with the Swedish Trade Union Confederation (LO), and approximately 70% of the office personnel belong to the Central Organization of Salaried Employees (TCO), the largest union for white-collar employees. The Swedish Employers Confederation (SAF) represents around 80% of the country's employers in the private sector.

The "federation" principle is applied. This means that, in one of Ericsson's units for example, all the factory workers are represented by the Metal Workers Union (Metall), all the Ericsson production foremen are represented by the Swedish Supervisors Union (SALF), and office employees are represented by the Swedish Industrial Salaried Employees Union (SIF) or by the Union of Graduate Engineers (CF). Thus, each Ericsson unit has to work out its own agreement with employees, based on local application of the contracts agreed upon by management and labor at the national level. Each unit also has to observe all the laws pertaining to joint consultation, negotiation, etc., that apply to each union organization.

The unions are represented on Ericsson's board of directors by two members and two deputy members, who are also entitled to attend board meetings and express their views. As a result, it is possible for all the major unions to be represented, to obtain insight into company policies and operations and to influence the decisions taken. Prior to each board meeting—in Ericsson, at least—all current matters are reviewed with the union representatives on the board.

Union representatives on boards of directors have not played the major role that was anticipated for them, partly because virtually all matters affecting employees are governed by the Codetermination Act and, accordingly, are negotiated at other levels within an organization.

Each major Ericsson unit in the Swedish sector of the Group has another body—the Works Council, consisting of representatives of management and the unions—which serves as a vehicle for information and consultation but which has no decision-making power. These councils meet quarterly but normally have working committees—concerned with such matters as production, safety, and employee proposals—that meet monthly. The value of the councils and the working committees to the average employee depends to a large degree on the competence and diligence of the union representatives.

In actual practice, the compulsory consultation and negotiation requirements of the Codetermination Act are creating problems in maintaining contact with employees. This applies particularly to middle management, since the union has to have advance information on all changes before such proposals can be discussed openly. It occasionally happens that information reaches a manager's subordinates, via the union, even before the manager has been informed and has been able to discuss the matter with his associates. Regular meetings between top management and middle management offer one way of partially preventing such unfortunate occurrences.

The closest contact between representatives of management and the individual employees takes place in the so-called "shop floor groups." In these groups, foremen and workers—who participate on a rotating basis—meet at regular intervals for consultation and discussion related directly to the workplace. Questions covered deal with production, changes in products, methods, and equipment, job transfers, etc., and the employee can have a direct influence on his work situation.

As is the case in other Swedish companies, we attach great importance to this mode of participation. To have motivated and interested employees—and this applies also to office employees—it is extremely important to give them the information, training, and participatory influence that they require. To this end it is equally important to establish good day-to-day contacts and a relationship of trust and confidence between supervisors and their workers.

In this context the new Development Agreement offers great promise. It gives all parties involved a possibility of finding shorter, smoother contact routes between management and the employees who are directly involved in specific operations. It also offers an approach that can be adapted to the conditions and requirements of individual companies.

Evidence is emerging that the spirit of mutual management–labor trust that was expressed in the Swedish model of the 1950s is still a powerful force that can be mobilized in behalf of increased productivity.

The rapid pace of technical development within our field of telecommunications has recently forced us to restructure our operations from top to bottom in a manner that has affected virtually every employee. The emphasis now is on electronic systems and equipment, rather than electromechanical production. We are using computers for both design and manufacturing operations, and because our new systems are capital-intensive rather than labor-intensive, we have had to reduce our work force despite very substantial increases in sales volume.

This massive changeover, with its inevitable impact on the lives of many employees, would not have been possible except for three factors:

- responsible awareness on the part of the unions and their representatives that their stake in the future of the company was as great as management's;
- a comprehensive and detailed program of information and consultation that clarified what had to be done, proposals to do it, and its contribution to Ericsson's competitiveness in world markets;
- competent and understanding managers who had established good contacts with employees at all levels of the company, and who were able to motivate them to make unusual efforts.

CONCLUSION

It is not necessary to stress that external laws and regulations are not needed to obtain the kind of cooperation we achieved. It stemmed from something internal: a spirit of loyalty to our company and to what it stands for, an appreciation of the stakes involved, and an atmosphere of mutual confidence and trust.

We live in an age in which great progress has been made in improving the quality of life for employees in virtually all industrialized countries. Workplaces are cleaner and safer. Robots and other forms of automation are removing much of the heavy and monotonous work from industrial processes. High wages and salaries provide common access to material goods that would have been considered fantastic luxuries only a few generations ago. Extended holidays give employees more leisure in which to enjoy their possessions and enrich their personal lives.

A vital prerequisite for further improvement will continue to be a company's profitable operation and development. Without such growth—which cannot be achieved without continuing increases in productivity—it is unrealistic to expect that industrial organizations can meet the rising expectations of employees, stockholders, or society as a whole.

The challenge to increase productivity is probably the most serious one facing management and labor today. It also happens to be the one that offers the greatest immediate and long-term rewards.

Labor–Management Relations in a New Technological Environment

SOICHIRO ASANO

President
Japanese Metal Industrial Workers' Union
Japan

LABOR UNION IN RESPONSE
TO TECHNOLOGICAL INNOVATION

Remarkable technological innovation was a key underpinning to the rapid economic growth Japan achieved from 1955 to 1965. Democratic labor unions in Japan willingly responded to this development, while enterprises established management consultation meetings and utilized this progressive technical revolution to democratize management and secure industrial democracy. In this environment, a prior consultation system was employed in which labor agreements were to be signed regarding the formulation and implementation of detailed plans and distribution of profits.

It is said that labor unions in Japan essentially are enterprise unions, because only one union exists in a given enterprise. Usually the labor union as one body comprises white-collar workers and blue-collar workers, even blue-collar workers with various jobs. Workers feel that they are employees and at the same time union members—they are conscious of belonging to an enterprise and labor union concurrently. Workers cooperate for the development of enterprises and some union members are even promoted to managerial posts and directorships.

The general employees (union members) are committed to secure employment opportunities, thus contributing to the improvement of labor conditions and the prosperity of the enterprise. In other words, employees are actively involved in developing enterprises and improving their achievements.

Confrontation between management and labor can occur, but labor and management work on equal terms, each recognizing their respective personalities. This relationship is sustained by mutual trust between labor and management. As for collective bargaining, a labor union from an enterprise participates in the bargaining with that enterprise's management. It is common that the decision

51

made in collective bargaining can be implemented by all the employees. As a consequence, labor agreements and work regulations can be applied through one channel.

Employee transfer to another work location or to a different kind of work as a result of technological innovation has been made smoothly through labor and management consultation. The changes involved in technological innovation have been facilitated remarkably by labor and management cooperation. What is particularly pertinent is that Japan has adopted a lifetime employment system. If a worker has the motivation and aptitude for the work, he is allowed to work in the same enterprise until retirement. This indicates that there is no layoff system (temporary layoff system) as is observed in many other countries. The Japanese people's strong work ethic and sense of pride in their work have also allowed for an easier transition.

Regarding the question of the higher education system, Japanese people receive compulsory education for nine years until junior high school, accounting for nearly 100% of school attendance. Furthermore, 90% of them enter senior high school for three years. It must be mentioned that the average education in Japan is comparatively higher than the world standard. Those students graduating junior high schools and senior high schools become blue-collar workers. Some enterprises provide the employees with in-service training consisting of technical instruction on a junior college level. These middle echelon employees frequently become foremen, facilitating work at their workshop. And most play an important role as union members.

The wage system is primarily based on seniority, while recently new wage systems based on crafts and jobs have been partially introduced. These wage systems guarantee the workers a stable lifetime employment and income and allow them to plan their future lives as long as they work honestly. At the time of mandatory retirement specified under the age limit, a lump-sum retirement allowance equivalent of 40 to 50 months pay is provided.

Japanese labor and management relations have many useful aspects that differ from those of other countries. For example, the Japanese labor movement has been striving for the preservation of sound and stable labor and management relations by respecting the principles of freedom, peace, and democracy.

RESPONSE TO MICROELECTRONICS (ME): THE THIRD INDUSTRIAL REVOLUTION

(1) The reasons for diffusion of microelectronics:

- Enterprises strive to improve productivity and to restrain cost increases. The main objective of introducing robots is to save labor, improve productivity, and reduce cost, which tend to enhance the competitive edge of products.

- Advancement of ME technology and improvement of economic efficiency by robots. The improved economic efficiency and reliability of robots are attributed to the rapid expansion of ME technology, which in turn has realized higher-quality products at lower cost. The rising cost of labor has further provided the economic justification of robot introduction.
- Robots have been widely introduced to solve labor shortages and to improve safety measures. Labor shortages occurred in the small- and medium-sized enterprises in the automobile and electric sectors due to production increases. A shortage of frontline workers arose from the phenomenon of an aging society and from higher educational achievement. Robots are also used to save workers from hazardous work such as welding and painting under adverse working conditions.

(2)   General impact of the ME revolution:

- Efforts should be focused on minimizing employment repercussions. The lessons of the first industrial revolution should be recognized and the necessary preliminary measures and adjustments should be strongly urged. Technological progress should not displace labor and at the same time generate difficult social problems. It is impossible to predict the social implications arising from the rapid permeation and unrestricted use of ME in every phase of people's lives. The creation of new employment opportunities and a fair apportionment of the results of productivity increases are strongly needed in order to alleviate workers' anxieties over job loss and work changes.
- Displacement of labor may occur in production work, clerical work, information processing, and inspection work sectors, which have been the major absorbers of labor until now.

(3)   ME on the international scene:

- The ME-related technological gap is broadening among the advanced countries and between advanced countries on the one hand and the developing countries on the other.
- New products, with improved performance and reduced cost, will affect adversely the price competitiveness of the existing products of the countries importing these new products. This in turn may jeopardize their existing industries.

(4)   Impacts of ME in Japan: The relatively limited incidence of employment problems so far has not given rise to a major controversy. However, since at present the introduction and application of ME technology are pervasive in every sector of the economy, labor unions should consider ways to cope with the consequent ramifications of the ME revolution.

- ME technology has been developed in an attempt to save labor, resources, and cost. Machines using ME will therefore replace human labor, as can actually be seen in the cases of NC machine tools and robots. Hence it is feared that ME may displace workers and increase unemployment. However, the resilience and flexibility of the Japanese socioeconomic–cultural system does not allow us, at the present stage, to predict a future incidence of employment problems on a massive level.

• The issue of the widening gap among different industries and enterprises caused by the progress of technological innovation arises. The ME revolution can spectacularly boost production efficiency. Those enterprises that have succeeded in introducing ME processes have boasted their potential for rapid growth. Small- and medium-sized enterprises, though, could encounter serious financial and manpower risks when they attempt to introduce ME. They must therefore proceed with due caution.

• The ME revolution gives rise to specialization and diversification of labor. The need for simple skilled workers will decline while that for highly skilled professional and simple unskilled workers (part-time workers) will increase. Also, the proportion and importance of people involved in technical repair work and clerically skilled work (such as service and sales) will increase relative to production workers.

• The issue of changing values comes to the fore. For instance, workers must duly anticipate that the skills developed through long experience and training in a firm could be rendered meaningless by some newly introduced technology. This implies denial of certain values instilled through experience or long years of service. Until some new values emerge tensions may continue.

• It seems that the advent of the aging society parallel to the progress of the ME revolution will affect markedly the workshop, skill, and training.

(5) Surveys to measure influence of ME in Japan: Such surveys have been conducted mainly from the perspective of employment by the following organizations: the Ministry of Labor, Japan Association of Information Processing Development, Japan Committee for Economic Development, Japan Productivity Center, Japan Federation of Labor, IMF-JC, All-Japan Federation of Electric Machine Workers Unions, Federation of Japan Automobile Workers Unions, and National Federation of Metal Industry Trade Unions. The general findings indicate:

• ME is widely used and rapidly spreading.

• For the time being, ME does not affect employment seriously. In the future, however, full measures will be necessary to cope with its impact. Such measures will require additional surveys and examinations.

The survey conducted by the National Federation of Metal Industry Trade Unions found the following:

- Increase or decrease of full-time employees: The rate of decrease in man-ufacturing sectors was 1–9%. Meanwhile in the area of OA machine opera-tions, and conversely in the clerical administrative sectors, an increase of 1–9% has been observed.
- Reassignment, job transfer, changes of employment conditions: The work-ers replaced by robots are in most cases transferred to other departments. The predominant majority of the specialists involved with robots and OA are under the age of 29.
- Reactions of union members: Criticism against robot introduction was scarcely heard. Rather, at the moment, reactions are not very tangible, probably because no one can foretell the future direction of technological innovation.
- Psychological impact on workers: During the initial phase of robot introduc-tion, both young and middle-aged/elderly workers indicated a certain fa-tigue and stress. The younger workers with more adaptability show quick recovery.

(6)   Some measures proposed by labor unions:

- Expansion and improvement of survey and research systems.
- Encouragement of labor unions' participation in policy formulation at the levels of enterprises, industries, local governments, and the national gov-ernment in an effort to establish industrial democracy.
- Improvement of functions of labor—management consultation. Such con-sultation should cover basic management policy, production, and equip-ment planning. As for the introduction of industrial robots, prior in-depth labor—management consultation and a resulting consensus must be the prerequisite.
- The functions of labor—management meetings at the industrial levels must be enhanced.
- The positive gains realized through the introduction of robots must be reflected in the expansion of employment opportunities, increase of in-come, and improvement of national welfare. A considerable portion of the benefits should be translated into reduced work hours.
- All necessary measures must be taken to protect workers from feelings of alienation from and disorientation of their value systems.
- Complete overhaul of in-house, outside, and public vocational training systems to improve and develop workers' abilities.
- Regarding the physical and psychological consequences on the workers caused by the introduction of ME, proper standards of labor safety and hygiene based on labor science must be established.
- To avoid further international conflict, full consideration should be given to joint international development of new technology and exchanges of infor-

mation. The labor unions, on their part, should further strengthen their ties with internationally organized labor movements.

In summary, the greatest importance is attached to employment security and the principles of coexistence of labor and technology, humanization of labor, and improvement of workers' living standards.

PART 2

Productivity Measurement and Improvement

Productivity Scheme: A Case Study in Blue Circle Industries PLC

R. B. FREEMAN

Manager, Group Personnel
Blue Circle Industries PLC
United Kingdom

Productivity needs to be defined before its measurement and management can be considered. Labor productivity (output per person) is the narrowest definition, but it is incomplete since the purpose of an entire enterprise is to be as productive as possible and labor is only part of the equation. It tends also to be a declining part of the equation as modern technology, automation, and robotics become more widely accepted and integrated.

My definition of productivity is the "ratio" between output and all the factors employed to create that output: raw materials, consumables, direct labor, plant and equipment, energy, fixed costs, etc. Of course, this relationship cannot be varied by waving a magic wand. It is essential to involve all levels of employees in productivity improvement to create a climate in which improvements can be optimized. After all, those who do the work can often make a highly valuable contribution to the problems that management wrestles with every day. The management of productivity means, at the end of the day, the management of profitability, for one helps to determine the other.

Productivity is a determinant of profitability but it is not the only determinant; indeed, profit may even rise at a time when productivity falls. If, for example, the market allows for substantial price increases, profit and return on capital may appear healthy. However, the company's efficiency at converting its inputs to outputs may be worsening and the longer-term prospects for profit may be degenerating. Only productivity measurement provides a company with the basis for controlling the operation's real efficiency. Understanding this is just as important at junior supervisory levels as at senior levels of the company.

Management by productivity may be said to be based on the premise that if you look after the efficiency factors the costs will look after themselves. To illustrate this, neither the directors nor the managers or supervisors of a company have any real control of the price of a unit of electricity. They do, however, control the amount of electricity used for each unit of output, and by reducing waste (idle motors running, plant operating below capacity, etc.) they can reduce the consumption of electricity per unit of output and thereby reduce the cost, generating increased profit or the opportunity to increase volume by controlling prices.

It is essential in any method of management of productivity that *all the elements* involved in producing the final units of output are taken into account. This means that plant and machine productivity must be measured as well as the consumption of indirect labor and other fixed costs in order to achieve an overall picture of the enterprise's true efficiency.

There must be a basis of comparison in order to establish whether productivity is rising or falling. This, of course, can be done on a period-by-period basis; it can also be done by developing figures for a base time period (normally a previous trading year thought to be reasonably efficient). A third approach is by the use of productivity standards or targets created in advance and recognized as achievable. Whatever form of comparison is used, it is important to evaluate productivity not only on a period-by-period basis but also as a trend over a specific span, since one period can obviously be misleading.

The purpose of managing productivity effectively is not only to achieve the best use of labor resources, but also to optimize capacity utilization, raw material conversion rates, energy consumption, and other factors involved in the company's manufacturing process. Using productivity information often provides a basis for improved corporate and strategic planning, particularly with respect to plant investment, expansion or contraction, rationalization, and so forth.

Many of the U.K.'s traditionally managed companies have tended to restrict their attempts to improve productivity by shedding labor and introducing modern equipment. In the recent recession, this became a predominant approach, obscuring or neglecting not only many other important elements in the productivity mix, e.g., cost reductions in materials, services, and/or methods, but also the need to obtain a real interest in and commitment to productivity gains from the work force, rather than mere accommodation to help preserve jobs.

One large manufacturer injected substantial new investment in future design, but this very same company states that its productivity, although it has closed the gap behind others in Europe, still lies woefully short of matching the Japanese. The preoccupation with new technology and labor reductions as the ultimate way to improve productivity is proving in practice to be at least a partial failure. This approach to the problem is unbalanced. By tackling productivity this way while neglecting the vital element of the work force's commitment to change defeats the ultimate aim. The philosophy of improving productivity should embrace all factors, including the morale and attitude and flexibility of the work force.

It is generally recognized that the Japanese approach to treating employees as a family coupled with the Japanese employees' commitment to company and country, ahead of even the family, results in a far greater degree of employee commitment and motivation. Europeans now believe that they will never be able to compete fully with the Japanese on this particular basis. It is interesting to notice that when the Japanese have established factories in the U.K., they have introduced many of their participative techniques, particularly their management style and their sensitivity. The results have almost invariably been extremely successful.

PRODUCTIVITY OBJECTIVES: BLUE CIRCLE INDUSTRIES PLC

The company carried out studies in 1977–1978 to find the most appropriate ways of reflecting the true performance of its business interests in order to introduce a self-financing productivity scheme for its employees. Seventeen alternative concepts were evaluated against a number of critical factors which had to be satisfied. These factors considered the effects of the concepts on

- output,
- quality,
- ability to meet government guidelines,
- the work force and acceptability to it, and
- the company and the acceptability to it.

Five schemes satisfied all of these factors and were evaluated in further depth. Wide-ranging criteria considering operational, political, and cost aspects, were ranked to obtain a weighted judgment to be applied to each scheme. It was recommended that the added value scheme should be chosen for depth analysis and evaluation. Added value was eventually accepted by the board as meeting all the specified criteria. An integral part of these studies was the establishment of a working party of senior managers to contribute to the design of the scheme in order to ensure management commitment and workability.

The scheme covered two main areas: (1) productivity payments for real increases in productivity, i.e., wealth sharing, and (2) participation and employee involvement.

The *primary* objectives were to

- improve productivity,
- strengthen and encourage genuine employee involvement,
- improve communications,
- increase understanding of the business,
- stabilize industrial relations, and
- create the environment for introducing change.

Productivity Payments

The formula chosen to measure true productivity performance of our particular business was based on the added value concept, and the total costs of running the business were reflected in the following formula:

	Base month	Current month
Sales value	100	106.6
Less purchase of materials, fuels, power, services, and fixed costs of running the company	66.5	67.3
= Added value	33.5	39.3
Divided by wages, salaries, employee costs and benefits, plus depreciation of fixed assets at replacement values	26.7	27.7
Gives productivity factor	1.25	1.42
Improvement		13.6%
Employees' share of improvement (of the % improvement)		10.2%

The formula was tested using the previous five years' performance before it was presented to the government. At that time, the government had applied a wages and prices freeze across industry. In five months of negotiation with government departments, the formula, which reflected genuine productivity improvements, was accepted.

The formula took into account the total costs of running the business. It produced an added value into which was divided the total resources of the business, the total resources being the plant, buildings, and machines depreciated at replacement values, together with total employee costs. By dividing the added value created by the total resources of the business consumed, a productivity factor was created for the actual period. Productivity factors were calculated for each month of a 12-month base period. This was established as the 12 months from July 1977 through June 1978. These periods were seasonally adjusted to smooth out peaks and troughs and are used as a benchmark to assess future productivity improvements.

The productivity factor from the appropriate base period is compared with the productivity factor in the actual period under review. Any increase in the productivity factor is applied to a payment formula:

$$\text{average of all basic wages/salaries} \times \text{75\% of the \% improvement in the productivity factor} \times \frac{\text{number of shifts/days worked}}{\text{number of shifts/days required to be worked}} = \text{employees' productivity payment}$$

The company, of course, also benefited since the scheme was designed to protect the profit margins. We paid for genuine productivity improvements and not for increased added value.

Participation and Employee Involvement

Around this formula a national agreement was devised, which was negotiated over 12 months with the unions concerned. Within this agreement there was a structure for participation and employee involvement throughout the U.K. covering in excess of 70 locations and 12,000 employees. Having achieved agreement with the national unions, management now had to communicate details of the scheme throughout its many locations in the U.K. For this reason, they devised a package of introduction to employees, which consisted of 16-mm color films, slide/tape presentations, a management guide, and an employee handbook. Teams of professionals introduced this to all locations in the company and a value added package was given to every major unit. In the first 12 months, 109 individual professional presentations took place by the teams. Factory management personnel, having been involved in the first presentation, were then involved in carrying the message through their own hierarchy to every employee in that plant.

The national unions nominated participants (*not* representatives) to join with management participants in their local productivity groups. This was a major breakthrough: for the first time all trade unions, both blue and white collar, agreed to sit around the same table and discuss problems together as a group. Each productivity group consisted of a mixture of management and union nominees, who were trained to act as a group and as thinking, creative individuals, rather than as representatives of individual interest groups.

THE PRODUCTIVITY GROUP

The size of the productivity group was determined by the number of recognized trade unions in the factory, as each union nominated a participant to sit on the local group. Since each union basically represented a separate skill, we had up to seven participants with varying backgrounds. Management then nominated one participant for every union participant and used a vertical slice of the management hierarchy to ensure involvement at all levels. Disciplines were also taken into account. The General Manager of the factory was the chairman and counted as one of the management participants. No voting was allowed: consensus was the aim. The training courses covered the new "role of the participant" and "consensus seeking."

The Function of the Productivity Group

The productivity group had the following functions:

- prepare, monitor, and review the unit's productivity plans,
- consider the monthly productivity scheme information,

- encourage managers, supervisors, and employees jointly to develop productivity ideas,
- make recommendations for possible improvements or cost savings,
- examine areas of the operation to identify opportunities to increase efficiency,
- investigate inefficient and wasteful practices to effect savings, and
- provide information to employees at the unit on the operation of the scheme and productivity matters.

This then gives a picture of a typical productivity group.

Attitudes and Training

In devising the productivity agreement, considerable thought was given to the various attitudes of employees, and judgments were made as to the expected reactions of different groups. These judgments were tabulated and used when devising the necessary training and education program. For example:

Question: What will management's reaction be to involving employees in local decision-making at the factories?

Anticipated answers:

- Resistance: We are paid to manage; they have little to offer.
- It will reduce our status and authority.
- It will mean telling them more about the business—financial and production figures. We have never done that before.
- They will know as much as we do.

Question: What will the union representatives' reaction be to becoming involved in local decision-making?

Anticipated answers:

- Good: we shall demand to see all the costs of the business.
- We shall show them how to manage.
- We shall demand full disclosure of all information on future plans, investment, etc.

Many of the projected responses were, in fact, correct. The prior analysis enabled an approach to be developed that constructively responded to these attitudes.

Course I Objectives

A substantial education/training program for the 44 groups was undertaken, consisting of residential courses for each productivity group, management and union participants together. The first one-week course was entitled "How a Business Works" and was a computer-based workshop. At the end of the course, the participants would be able to:

- explain what role a business fulfills and how the individual contributes to that role;
- describe and discuss the various functions that make up an enterprise;
- explain how an enterprise fits into the community and economy as a whole;
- list the important areas of policy in which a company must plan for the future to provide for its workers, shareholders, and customers;
- read a company balance sheet and profit and loss statement, identifying salient features, and discuss the performance of the business; and
- decide, given basic financial and economic information, on possible strategies to be adopted by an enterprise to meet its objectives.

Course II Objectives

A second one-week course was undertaken some two months later at which the same groups went through an interactive skills workshop. On completion of the training all productivity group members would have:

- recognized the potential range of benefits of the scheme and discussed fully any concerns they prompted;
- examined the implications of their membership in the productivity group to their own managerial/representative role and started to resolve any concerns they may have about it;
- become more knowledgeable and experienced in those skills which they need to play their parts effectively in the productivity group, such as problem-solving skills, communication skills, consensus seeking, opportunity thinking.

Both courses used a number of general core modules: role analysis, principles of communication, problem-solving techniques, opportunity thinking, management of meetings, interpersonal communication skills, and program planning. A unique feature of this training and education program was that the trainer involved in conducting the workshops then became the counselor for that productivity group once the participants were back on site in their factories. This was to help the members sustain the skills in the new role that they had developed.

Disclosure of Information

A further important feature of ensuring a commitment to improved productivity by these local groups was to secure a policy from the highest level on disclosure of information. Disclosure can be difficult in certain circumstances, particularly regarding price-sensitive information, for example. Nevertheless, a policy was agreed upon and a system was designed that was complementary to the productivity scheme's added value formula.

The system devised was a data analysis by ratio and trend (DART). This system took the 14 most critical ratios in running our business, which were produced on a monthly basis for each unit, each area, and for the company as a whole. Each of the 14 ratios showed the actual performance for the month and a trend graph for the previous months, and compared them to the base periods. By scanning these ratios, it was possible to identify very quickly those areas that were worthy of investigation to improve the efficient running of the factory. In effect it provided the productivity groups, who had been trained to focus their attention and skills on problem solving and creative thinking, with an opportunity to become involved and to participate in improved plant effectiveness.

PITFALLS AND FAILINGS OF U.K. MANAGEMENT

Some of the main problems experienced in such a major program were due in part to the British managers' ingrained style of resistance to change. Over the past two decades many new schemes have been tried in industry and have failed through lack of support by management. Each individual scheme, often imposed from the center, is viewed with suspicion and is generally expected to disappear within one to two years of introduction. Such schemes ranging from MBO (management by objectives) in the 1960s to today's QC (quality circles) are grasped with enthusiasm as the panacea for all our ills, and are quickly introduced without sufficient research and planning. Consequently, they are generally unsuccessful.

Productivity through employee involvement is often cast into this mold. Since it is viewed by management as a threat to status and because it is difficult to quantify the benefits in tangible terms, management resistance to change can be guaranteed. Although prepared for this resistance, the time taken to change attitudes and management style was underestimated. The average middle-aged British manager has been brought up to expect and deal with conflict. An adversary situation is referred to regularly by management and unions. A change of attitude cannot be achieved readily. It may take many years of sustained efforts emanating from the top and reflected in all types of policies, procedures, and performance criteria.

Possibly the biggest mistake made in introducing this productivity scheme was underestimating the time required to gain all of management's commitment and the fact that the approach, having obtained board approval, was to start at the factory level and work upward through the organization. Some two years into the scheme it was necessary to go back to senior executives who had suffered through a lack of communication: The lower levels were losing impetus due to lack of obvious support from their peers.

CONCLUSIONS

It was estimated at the outset that it would take five to ten years before we could achieve all we were setting out to do in the participation field. However, when plans were laid some three to four years ago for this long-term program we could not have envisaged that there would be a world-wide recession on a massive scale. The U.K. has suffered and my own company has had to reduce labor and capacity, but has taken those steps after careful thought, consultation, and indeed involvement at the factory level in implementing these plans. To some, this was the death knell of the productivity scheme and employee involvement program, but they were wrong.

In fact, the effect of the recession has brought forth a new comprehension of the realities that our company and industry in general are facing. The training and education program that employees underwent played some part in this new understanding.

The productivity groups are still functioning, and because of the drop in sales volume due to shrinking markets, the payment side of the productivity scheme has not produced the tangible results that were hoped for. Nevertheless, the groups continue to function with the objective of ensuring that their plants are viable to protect the job security of those still employed. A new spirit of realism has been created.

One of the positive results that has emerged is that because of the massive training program giving greater understanding of how the business works and a greater realism of the ravages inflicted by the recession, subjects that in past years may have been taboo are now faced openly. They are discussed in mixed groups of employees, which is something many of us never envisaged would take place.

We know that we are now in a better position to take advantage of any upturn in the marketplace. We know that we are also in a better position with the understanding and commitment of our employees. We know that the path we took to introduce a true measure of productivity within our company and to share any increased gains fairly among all our employees will stand us in good stead for the years ahead, both competitively in the U.K. and Europe and in the world markets. The longer-term benefits from involving employees in the business they give their lives to will far outweigh short-term benefits.

The objective of a truly committed and enthusiastic work force cannot be fully achieved by an involvement-based productivity scheme while other personnel policies act to divide employees. In the U.K., it has been traditional for many years for shop floor employees to have substantially inferior conditions of employment than other staff.

Our company's personnel planning is based on the gradual removal of these ''indefensible differentials'' as a matter of corporate philosophy. We believe that industry generally will not achieve a sense of common purpose or total employee commitment while maintaining artificial barriers, which are themselves partly responsible for some of the problems we face today.

Full employee commitment to a company's objectives and the full utilization of productivity opportunities will only begin to be achieved when individuals believe that their treatment is fair and just in terms of rewards and dignity.

White-Collar Productivity Measurement

KENNETH A. CHARON

Group Director
Operation Planning Information Systems and Communications Group
IBM Corporation
United States

In analyzing the ingredients of a successful productivity program, the same set of fundamentals applies, regardless of geography, industry, or company. The approach and specific measurement system presented here was first adopted in IBM Europe. The measurement system has since been implemented throughout the IBM Corporation under the name "functional productivity system," and can be envisioned as useful across a worldwide organization.

The fundamental factors affecting productivity are as follows:

- capital investments,
- R&D expenditures,
- innovative uses of new technologies,
- motivation of human resources—employees and management, and finally
- management.

Within this final, obvious, but yet most forgotten fundamental, the stress should be on organization geared to productivity and measurements as the most vital tools of management.

Another very important factor that transcends the five fundamentals is the drastic change in the composition of the labor force in the industrialized nations of the world.

LABOR FORCE COMPOSITION

A number of important changes in the U.S. workforce have occurred over the period 1860–1980:

- The reduction in the agricultural work force has been dramatic, while food production has increased even more dramatically. This is a result of the productivity made possible primarily by technological progress.

- Manufacturing industry employment was relatively stable until the post-World War II period, when technology and improved production methods brought about reductions.
- Employment in the service industries, such as banking and insurance, has been on a steady increase since 1960, after a century of relative stability.
- Most startling is the emergence and steady growth of employment in the fields of information creation, recording, processing, and distribution.

These profiles have many implications, but for the purpose of relating employment trends to productivity, the most salient considerations are:

(1)   The impacts of technology on productivity.

(2)   The significant and continuing shift of labor away from the high-productivity sectors—industry and agriculture—where productivity is most understood.

(3)   The incredible growth of the service and information sectors, where productivity is least understood.

(4)   The need to understand the long-range effects of these shifts on national economic goals.

(5)   The tremendous impacts that these shifts within the labor force have had in bringing confusion to the subject of productivity measurements. As long as manufacturing industries were the leading employers, we could use their productivity indicators as reasonably representative of the total. This is no longer true.

THE PRODUCTIVITY CHALLENGE

These shifts in the work force have important consequences for governments, industries, and companies:

(1)   The tremendous challenge for retraining: retraining farm workers to become factory assemblers was not difficult; retraining steel mill workers and factory assemblers to become computer programmers is a much greater challenge.

(2)   The fact that growth in the information sector, and to a certain extent the service sector, does not appear to be constrained by demand, but rather by skill availability, which again puts emphasis on training and education.

(3)   The urgency with which the service and information sectors must recognize the burden they now assume for attacking and solving the productivity challenge: They must make their current critical skills more productive to achieve the full growth potential available to them, and by so doing to absorb the retrained workers moving from manufacturing and agriculture.

Being part of those sectors, both as a provider of productivity tools to all sectors and as a large employer within the information sector, IBM has tried to respond to this challenge. The approach to productivity within IBM is outlined here as a means of demonstrating the importance of the fifth fundamental factor affecting productivity—management.

The emphasis on productivity must become a basic management responsibility, and there must be a formal role assigned for the coordination of productivity programs embedded in the organization. The most difficult challenge is to create a proper understanding at all levels of the company, and to do this in a credible way. Responsible approaches to productivity improvement cannot be based upon taxing finite resources with ever-increasing workloads. In fact, these efforts must be based upon better organization, better techniques, and more creative approaches to the job.

What productivity is—making the most efficient use of available resources—is quite a different matter. Basically, there are several ways in which this can be done: (1) by removing the unnecessary workload, (2) by reducing the necessary workload, and (3) by balancing resources and tools to deal efficiently with the legitimate workload that remains.

Until recently, productivity programs and measurements were primarily associated with the manufacturing process. The industrial revolution brought with it great emphasis on production methods, efficient tooling, and productivity measurements. The industrial engineering profession was, in fact, born as a result of this emphasis and made a truly outstanding contribution to the production process. However, management of the nonmanufacturing parts of the business was slower to recognize similar opportunities. The result was omission or confusion as to approach and responsibilities in most companies.

IBM has attempted to recreate the industrial engineering approach to productivity in the white-collar areas of its business. This approach is based upon the following:

- understanding the need for action (IBM's executives spend a great deal of time on this),
- creating a support organization that focuses on indirect manpower productivity programs,
- recognizing the need for cross-functional approaches and dependencies—a point too often overlooked and a weakness of most corporate management systems,
- reorienting our major investments toward productivity,
- streamlining and simplifying procedures to offset the impact of the growing complexities in our business,
- educating with productivity in mind,
- initiating productivity research to enhance understanding of the key factors that affect indirect productivity, and
- establishing a measurement system.

It became clear in late 1977 that we had to have an indirect workload measurement system. A task force was appointed which identified the following essential characteristics of such a system:

- It must be simple and understandable. Measurement systems become unusable if they cannot be understood.
- It must be usable at all levels of the organization, from the branch office to the country headquarters and to the chairman's office. It must be seen as a management aid, and it must allow for comparisons of similar activities and the workload they generate.
- It must be transparent to the organizational structure so that valid comparisons can be made. Many approaches have been defeated because of organizational differences interfering with interpretation.
- It must have a sound database structure and permit tracking over time. It should also measure workload in meaningful terms.
- It should identify efficient and inefficient areas so that the reasons for the differences can be investigated. This is most important.

THE COMMON STAFFING SYSTEM

Our measurement system is called the *common staffing system* (CSS). It measures the relative productivity of all of our nonmanufacturing work force, which we refer to as an indirect population or, more simply, white-collar workers.

Although the CSS has now been installed throughout IBM under the name *functional productivity system,* this discussion refers to experiences in installing this system in IBM Europe, where we were first to attack the white-collar productivity measurement problem.

Some terms need clarification. First, in IBM, the term ''function'' is used in the broad, categorical sense to refer to a grouping of activities such as marketing, development, manufacturing, administration, personnel, or finance. The measurement system was designed to identify the relative productivity of similar functions. Second, although organizational structure may vary in different countries, the actual work performed is very similar in each country or in each IBM business unit, regardless of where it conducts it business. The system measured the productivity of 26,000 people whose work could be described by 135 written job activities and who were driven by 57 different causes of work.

Basic Approach

The first problem was to define *what* was being done. In our environment that meant that we had to define the specific activities of all 26,000 indirect resources and do it in such a way that it would be consistent between all countries as well as through time. Next, we had to identify *why* these activities were being done: what were the drivers and work causes. We ended up with 57 work causes.

Once the definitions were identified, periodic simultaneous surveys could be conducted across all functions in all countries to quantify the what and the why. Finally, the survey inputs from all countries were put together into one central data file for the productivity assessments.

Past attempts to capture what the 26,000 indirect resources were doing in a consistent manner were thwarted by the fact that each country had a different organization structure and used different terms to describe its various activities. In the CSS joint approach, 135 activities were defined that were performed in all countries and that could be compared for productivity. All functions and countries participated in selecting these activities and in defining them in sufficient detail to ensure that they described exactly what was intended to be covered by the activity—where it started, where it ended, and what terms were to be included so that each country's interpretation was consistent. Some examples of the 135 activities are:

- secretarial and typing support
- order entry
- accounts receivable

Fifty-seven different work causes were then identified (generally chosen to be readily auditable and forecastable), for example:

- The work cause "population" is used in relation to the activity "secretary and typing."
- The work cause "number of orders" is the major factor in the requirements for the activity "order entry."
- The work cause "number of points installed" (a measure of revenue) is the major factor for the activity "accounts receivable."

One of the problems in conducting the survey is to capture all of the resources performing an activity within a country regardless of where and in how many different parts of the organization structure it really is being done. CSS has the facility to normalize these different organization structures, and we refer to this as providing "organization transparency."

We do this through a hypothetical organization that we call the "CSS model." Each of the 135 activities is placed into a *model function* that represents where it is most frequently done within the countries and where it most logically belongs. For example, the CSS model function called "administration" includes 12 of the 135 activities, such as activity 101, "order entry"; activity 102, "marketing support"; activity 103, "backlog management." The CSS model function "finance" includes 16 of 135 activities, such as "billing" and "accounts receivable." The model function approach is the vehicle that gives consistency and organizational transparency.

Thus far, the CSS approach includes 135 activities to define *what* and 57 work causes to identify *why,* with twice-yearly surveys to quantify these across all countries. Each time a survey database from all of our countries is compiled, productivity assessments are provided in three distinctly different ways:

(1) The first is a *comparison of the productivity* between each of the countries and country functions at that point in time.

(2) The second one is a procedure to *plan the productivity* in the future.

(3) The third is to *assess the productivity change* that has occurred in each country in this survey vs. the prior survey that we have done.

Productivity Comparisons

For an example of the productivity comparison, one of the 135 activities was called "order entry." Let us say that country A identified 10 indirect resources performing the activity "order entry" in our last survey. In other words, they had 10 equivalent people involved in that activity some place in their organization and it includes temporary, part-time, and subcontract personnel as well as IBM regular employees.

We have determined the major cause of effort for the activity "order entry" was thousands of orders processed. Let us say that country A had processed 10,000 orders with their 10 "order entry" resources for a ratio of one "order entry" person per 1000 orders processed. The next logical questions then are: Is that good or bad? Could it be improved?

Since the same information comes from 15 other countries, their productivity ratios for the "order entry" activity can now be determined to see if any pattern emerges. The problem has, in effect, been transformed into an opportunity. A single approach was designed to be applicable across 16 different countries of widely divergent sizes, organization structures, and geographic locations. This initially complex problem is now an opportunity to gain some valuable insights into productivity.

The base for comparison of country productivity is the weighted ratio for all countries and we call it the *norm ratio*. It is the sum of all "order entry" resources in the 16 countries divided by the sum of all their orders, which is shown in Fig. 1 on the sloping line. Those countries, such as country A, that have a ratio larger than the norm ratio (above the line) should try to understand why they require more "order entry" resources to process 1000 orders than the average country requires. Also, since country C appears to have the best productivity ratio of all, they should be able to provide some valuable guidance to the others.

Now, perhaps, some light is being shed on questions asked earlier: Is the productivity ratio for country A good or bad? Can it be improved? We see from

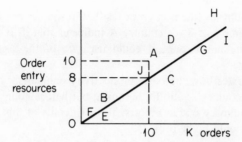

FIGURE 1. The norm ratio: the comparison of productivity by country.

this example that if country A had a productivity ratio equal to the norm ratio, it would only require eight resources for "order entry" instead of the 10 it has and could use the additional two resources in a more critical area.

Of course, it may be that there are valid reasons for some (or even all) of this difference in country A, but that will be determined when we follow through on these measurements and understand how other countries perform their "order entry" operations—more on this point later.

The relative productivity is likewise compared to the average for each of the 135 activities for each of the 16 countries, just as was done in the "order entry" example.

The last step in the technique is to generate summaries of these 135 results to provide productivity comparisons for various organization levels. These include activity, function, country, and unit summaries.

The activity summary (Table I) is a listing of the productivity comparison data and results for each country for one activity, such as the "order entry" example. As already shown, country A has an actual resource of 10 man-years of effort performing "order entry" and processed 10,000 orders for a productivity ratio of one resource per 1000 orders. Country B has a productivity ratio of 0.91, and the ratio for country C is 0.50—twice as good as country A. The average productivi-

TABLE I
CSS Activity Summary: Activity 101—"Order Entry" vs. K Orders

Country	Actual Resources	K Orders	Productivity Ratio	Norm Resources
A	10	10.0	1.00	8
B	5	5.5	0.91	4
C	7	14.0	0.50	11
⋮	⋮	⋮	⋮	⋮
Total	100	125.0	0.80	100

ty ratio for all countries (the norm ratio) is 0.80 resources per 1000 orders. Thus the ''norm resource'' of 8 for country A indicates that if its productivity ratio were equal to the norm ratio, it could use two of these resources in other activities.

This demonstrates how the basic productivity comparisons are generated by comparing each country's ratio to the norm; but before going on with explanations of other summary output reports, further details of this particular ''order entry'' activity would be helpful.

In fact, this happens to be a real example from the CSS program. It turned out that country A was not yet on a teleprocessing system in the branch office and orders had to be completed manually, filed and retrieved manually, and mailed or carried to the consolidated ''order entry'' location. Country B had a teleprocessing system but did not have a mass-transaction capability, and required each order to be entered individually. Country C was the most productive country of all. It was the country whose administration system designer provided it with a teleprocessing system having a mass-transaction capability permitting entry of 100 orders for the same customer at one time. It was agreed that all other countries would also adopt the system used by country C and when its implementation was released, a saving of approximately 200 man-years for ''order entry'' requirements was realized across Europe.

To return to the summary examples again, the function summary is intended to provide the manager of the function with the sum of the productivity comparisons for all of the activities in the area. The productivity comparison measurement for the total function is the sum of the activity results and, in Table II, it indicates that the 100 resources in administration would only be 90 if they had the average productivity on each of the activities.

These function summaries are actually put together in two ways: One is the summary of the results for all activities included in the CSS model function structure (as above) and another report summarizes the results for the activities within each of the actual organization functions in each country. The former is useful for the headquarters since it normalizes organization differences, but the

TABLE II
CSS Function Summary: Country A Administration Function

| Activity | Actual Resources | Norm | | Productivity Δ |
		Resources	Index	
101	10	8	1.25	+ 2
102	20	21	.95	− 1
:	:	:	:	:
:	:	:	:	:
Total	100	90	1.11	+10

TABLE III
CSS Country Summary: Country A

Function	Actual Resources	Norm Resources	Norm Index	Productivity Δ
Administration	100	90	1.11	+10
Finance	.	.	.	.
Personnel	.	.	.	.
Total	1000	920	1.09	+80

latter is essential to the countries since it gives the results for their real organization entities, which can be identified with management people for accountability and follow-up. This same procedure is used for the other, higher-level CSS summaries that will be mentioned.

The next level of summary is for the country. Each country general manager receives a one-page summary of the productivity measurement for each of the functional areas and this is aggregated to a total country result in the same fashion as was the function summary.

In total, as shown in Table III, the net result of adding all productivity changes in country A, for example, might indicate that they may have an opportunity to improve as much as 80 resources if they had the average productivity in all 135 activities. They could achieve this by attrition, by absorbing future growth without adding resources, or by some combination of the two. Of course, since the detailed reports tell the country general manager which activities and functions in the organization seem to have potential for improvement, resource requirements could be balanced among areas more equitably and placed where they can make the best contribution.

Likewise the summary of productivity comparison totals for each country provides a one-page report for the entire unit. The example in Table IV shows

TABLE IV
CSS Unit Summary: Unit Total

Country	Actual Resource	Norm Resource	Norm Index	Productivity Δ
A	1000	920	1.09	+80
B	.	.	.	.
C	.	.	.	.
Total	9000	9000	1.00	0 ·

9000 total resources, even though the survey total is actually 26,000. Naturally, since this is a summary of comparisons to the norm across all 135 activities and 16 countries, the plus and minus quantities are balanced at this level. That is, the total norm resource equals the total actual resource, the total norm index is 1.00, and the total productivity delta is 0.

What happens through time, of course, is that the productivity norms continuously improve since the emphasis is on those areas in each country where potential for improvement is indicated.

Productivity Planning

As mentioned before, each time a CSS survey is compiled the data are used for three separate productivity assessments. We have just seen the first of these, where productivity is compared between countries at one point in time. We look briefly now at the second one—"productivity planning."

The planning aspect is important because it is in the future that we can make things happen. The summary of productivity comparisons was interesting, but that was in the past and cannot be changed. The learning experience, however, should direct future efforts toward good resource planning in two ways: (1) the historical survey database should help to plan resource requirements more intelligently as a function of anticipated volume changes; (2) the productivity potentials identified should help to determine where and how much prospects can be improved.

The sample CSS survey database has provided useful information on the relationship between activity resources and the work cause quantity through the productivity ratios. If we can forecast the work cause quantity for some points in the future, we can use that ratio to determine what that change would do to resource requirements. In Fig. 2, for example, country A has 10 "order entry" resources to process 10,000 orders. If it plans to have 11,000 orders next year, then its productivity ratio of 1.00 would project a requirement of 11 "order

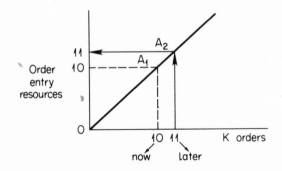

FIGURE 2. Using the norm ratio for forecasting by activity.

entry" resources next year *if* it continues at the same productivity level with no improvement. However, we have already seen from the last CSS productivity comparison that based on the norm it may have a potential improvement of two "order entry" resources; subsequent investigations have confirmed that it can in fact achieve this. Therefore, the plan for next year would include only 9 resources for "order entry" and one can be relieved for more critical jobs even though the country will process 1000 more orders next year than last. Further improvements could be reflected in the following year's plan.

These types of analyses can be done for each activity in each country and the results summarized to derive resource planning aids for higher organization levels such as function and country, just as shown in the productivity comparison technique.

These methods can provide management with a significant advantage previously lacking because the CSS concept, terms, and techniques are known and understood at all levels of the organization. This permits employees to work more effectively with the management team in a common language, more quickly evaluate the various inputs, ensure an aggressive but viable plan, and articulate that plan more intelligently and comprehensibly to superiors.

Productivity Tracking

The third use of the CSS database is productivity tracking. We have found where we have efficiencies and inefficiencies through the productivity comparisons, and that information can be utilized in formulating aggressive plans. The moment of truth comes then with the next CSS survey when we can measure the productivity improvements actually made and see if we have achieved our commitments.

The tracking technique compares, activity by activity, the productivity changes that each country has made between two consecutive CSS surveys. For example, in Fig. 3, if the CSS indicates that country A has moved from 10

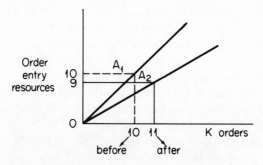

FIGURE 3. Using the norm ratio for tracking productivity.

"order entry" resources to process 10,000 orders in the last survey to only 9 resources for 11,000 orders in the current survey, then it has improved its productivity by approximately 20% and achieved its plan.

CSS Productivity Tracking reports can summarize these types of analyses for various organization levels, as was done in the other CSS assessments. The summaries are again provided by activity, function, country, and unit.

USES OF CSS IN IBM

An important point to realize is that the entire system is an open book within the company, and results for every country are distributed to all participants. Each manager being measured by the system must know not only where he has efficiencies and inefficiencies, but also how he fits into the total picture and where he might go to learn how to make improvements.

Reviews of the CSS results are also made for all management levels from the bottom to the top. These are handled by the CSS coordinators, as well as the function contacts, and their reviews include summaries, highlights of problem areas, and recommendations. After these reviews, the management of the areas can initiate follow-up action plans to understand why and what can be done.

In addition to all the CSS data and results, each participant also receives the names and phone numbers of the CSS people who coordinated the survey in the various countries to facilitate "cross-talk." A great amount of cross-talk occurs with each CSS publication, and it provides an excellent vehicle for improvement action. We have many examples of major productivity gains resulting from the use of very efficient techniques and programs in one business unit being spread to others as a result of the availability of CSS data throughout the company.

The "power of the published comparisons" is something mentioned earlier, but it deserves emphasis. If the productivity comparisons are reasonably fair and equitable, being compared to our peers can be an excellent vehicle to find out where improvements can be made and is a strong motivation to make changes where we compare unfavorably. We had strong support and use of this technique by virtually all countries and functions, and this is primarily because *they* have contributed to the design and consider it partly their tool. Each of us wants and deserves the opportunity to have some say in how we are measured and this involvement is the key to acceptance.

Another major advantage inherent in the CSS approach is as an aid to information systems investment. CSS can help to indicate which user areas of the business should have priority in the development of new information systems support programs by indicating probable productivity savings. This can help ensure that the program developments are justified and offer the maximum return on investments. After the fact, CSS can then assess how much of the expected improvement was achieved in the user area by the information systems implementation.

Indirect productivity measurement is far from a science. However, it is important to have a system, to work to improve it over time, and most important, to involve as many persons as possible in the productivity goals of the corporation.

PART 3

Productivity and
the Japanese Corporation

Corporate Management and Labor Relations in Japan

KOTARO TSUJIMURA

Professor of Economics
Keio University
Japan

MANAGEMENT SYSTEMS AND LABOR–MANAGEMENT RELATIONS

Recent years have seen a flurry of interest in the vigor of Japanese companies and in their capacity for raising productivity. Views have been heard from not a few overseas observers pointing to cultural traditions dating back an eon as the source of Japanese corporate vitality. Here "vitality" refers to companies' capacity for aggressively responding to market needs, as via new product development, high quality, reasonable pricing, quick delivery. Moreover, "market needs" include potential, cultivated and brought out through the development of new products.

To help shed some light on whether the distinctive characteristics of Japanese culture have in fact been behind the productivity gains realized in postwar Japan, a survey was conducted last year. In the questionnaire, executives and labor leaders were asked to cite the aspects of Japanese management that contributed to productivity gains and if these were unique to Japan. Responses to this questionnaire are summarized below.

1. Decision-Making

The point most often cited in regard to Japanese top management was that ultimate authority for both decision-making and execution is vested in the same body: namely, the board of directors or a corresponding group. Second, boards are comprised almost entirely of directors who have come up through the ranks in that company. Therefore, information on difficulties likely to occur in execution

85

is readily available at the decision-making stage; this greatly facilitates the implementation of decisions. Job rotation practiced in Japanese companies ensures that directors enjoy a common store of knowledge acquired through experience, and that their decision-making is based on sound understanding of the situations of respective divisions.

Another point made was that top management in Japan is concerned more with the long-range development of the company than with short-term earnings.

In most Japanese companies, top management initiates a decision process by issuing targets arranged in a general direction. Opinions and ideas from the different divisions are then sought and considered in the course of a multifaceted examination leading up to a final decision by top management. The effectiveness of this "U-turn" format derives in large part from the substantial authority it gives to office supervisors and floor foremen at the managerial terminus of the chain of command.

"Flexibility" is said to be a key feature of individual Japanese employees' approach to their work. Work parameters are loosely defined, and modes of execution are characterized by great flexibility. Ordinary employees share a common experiential outlook with their supervisors or foremen, who started out in the same kind of jobs as themselves. Work done by employees at various levels meshes excellently in a complementarity enhancing workplace efficiency.

U-turn decision-making amid this sort of organization gives all employees a sense of participation in and responsibility for decisions. It also serves to propagate understanding of the nature and intent of top management decisions. Even in large corporations, individual employees can thereby gain a clear understanding of the significance of their own individual work.

2. Personnel Practices

The decision-making and execution process described above is inseparably linked with a company's system for dealing with personnel. Perhaps the most important characteristic of Japanese personnel systems is in the area of advancement, where selection is a very long-term affair. This ensures fair and accurate evaluation and evokes general support for advancement decisions.

Another important characteristic is job rotation, which gives employees experience over a wide range of work. Job rotation enables employees to bring a broad outlook to their work and makes it easier for management to determine the right person (based on their performance in different kinds of work) for the right job. Employees become aware of their mutual complementarity and more easily adapt to technical progress.

A third characteristic is the practice of periodic, simultaneous hiring of new school leavers from various grades. Applicants are judged not so much on specialized knowledge or ability as on their potential, as seen in terms of drive, comprehension, and judgment.

3. Training

Intracompany education and training may be said to be major features of Japanese business. Companies often have a system of integrated training for new employees hired just out of school in the simultaneous, periodic hiring mentioned above. Both on-the-job training and classroom instruction by employee level are used, and the range of instruction can be very broad. As a result, employees are able to respond flexibly to market developments, technical progress, and other changes in the company's circumstances.

Still, most companies focus primarily on training on the job. Japanese work execution typically emphasizes complementarity among the capabilities of employees assigned to a particular shop at any given time. Meanwhile, on-the-job training is a superb vehicle for handing down detailed knowledge and skills that have been accumulated at a particular company. It is based on the recognition of the inadequacy of abstract manuals for conveying essential work-related concepts. It also helps employees to understand the nature of their role within the company.

4. Labor Unions

Besides the characteristics of Japanese management itself, the relationship between management and labor unions is also said to be a major contributing factor in company vitality. Practically all Japanese unions are company based and comprise both office workers and employees engaged directly in production. These unions have banded together into a number of large federations through which they cooperate with each other, but negotiations with management take place at the company level.

Not only is much information traded within a company's union, but joint meetings with management provide an opportunity for vigorously exchanging ideas and opinions. A meeting will be held, for instance, before the company introduces new equipment or modifies a production process. Hearing views from the different standpoints and reaching agreement beforehand may be an excellent way of ensuring smooth implementation of the measure in question. Furthermore, employees receiving general information from management and precise details through the union will have a solid understanding of new equipment, a new production process, etc.

Fourth, middle-level managers gradually elevated from the ranks of ordinary employees to positions of genuine responsibility can relate well with employees in their division and maintain a feeling of homogeneity.

5. Wages

Wage systems in Japanese companies are characterized first of all by a relatively weak correlation with the type of work performed, and a more positive correlation with seniority (e.g., retirement allowances are paid entirely by the company). These factors work in conjunction with job rotation and are helpful in minimizing employee turnover.

Second, bonuses account for a large share of total remuneration. The resultant flexibility of wage costs enables companies to maintain stable employment in the face of fluctuating sales. Bonuses also give employees a stake in company performance. They can be seen as a variant on profit-sharing systems long advocated in the West, and might be more effective where there are good labor–management relations to start with.

Third, wage differentials within companies are comparatively small. The pattern of Japan's postwar economic development has played a large role here, as has the vertical, company-based nature of Japanese labor unions.

"RATIONAL" CHOICES IN A GIVEN ENVIRONMENT

It is frequently pointed out that the characteristics of Japanese management and labor–management relations cited above as contributing to company vitality and productivity are not always found in the U.S. or Europe. These characteristics usually are explained as products of cultural traditions antedating modernization. Something that must be recognized, though, is that this is not actually the case.

Lifetime employment is clearly a precondition for all of the observed employment characteristics: homegrown management (from supervisors and foremen to members of the board), promotion based on long-term evaluation, heavy emphasis on intracompany education. However, it must be noted that lifetime employment did not see general application in Japan until the late 1950s, a fact confirmed by a white paper issued by Japan's Ministry of Labor in 1959 on the labor environment in Japan the preceding year.

The white paper attributed the relatively minor impact of the recession being experienced by Japan at the time on the labor environment to the increasing rigidity of employment and wages vis-à-vis economic fluctuations since the war, a rigidity the white paper claimed had not been seen in prewar recessions. By way of example, it described how a 6% shrinkage of production during the depression of 1929–1931 was accompanied by a 20% drop in employment and a 7% decline in wage scales (and thus a huge decline in total wage bill). The white paper traced the new rigidity of employment and wages to measures introduced after the war primarily by large corporations, including intracompany training for skilled workers, a commitment to the retention of key employees, and seniority-based wages.

Lifetime employment and the inseparably linked seniority-based wages were thus relatively new to Japan in the late 1950s. This kind of system evolved because of management efforts to adapt in the most reasonable fashion to prevailing economic conditions. Although Japan suffered from massive, disguised unemployment in the 1950s, there was also a critical shortage of skilled labor able to deal with the advanced technologies representing the state of the art in postwar world industry. Depending on the existing labor force of indigenous skill would never allow Japanese industry to catch up with its counterparts in the U.S. and Europe with new types of capital equipment. Members of management saw that the solution was to hire young graduates and train them within their companies. Since losing workers in midcareer would make it impossible to recoup this type of human investment, companies naturally set about devising ways to minimize turnover. To this end they turned to seniority-based wages, retirement allowances, and company-funded expansion of facilities for employee recreation and health care.

While it was in the 1960s that the need for manpower policies became apparent in the U.S., circumstances forced Japanese companies to make intensive investment in human capital in the 1950s. Japanese companies were predicating management policy on the basic complementarity between human and physical capital (of the new type) even before they had clearly conceptualized that complementarity as a principle.

Japan in the 1950s was highly influenced by the U.S., and it was from there that productivity campaigns and quality control systems were introduced into Japan. Nonetheless, the environment mentioned above kept the U.S. systems of temporary layoffs and job-based wages from gaining ground in Japan. Meanwhile, emphasis on the complementarity between physical and human capital led to recognition of the complementarity of capabilities among employees. Japanese companies in the 1950s and 1960s were far behind companies in developed nations of the West in the accumulation of plant and equipment. Management was left with no choice but to develop the use of human capital in order to compensate for this insufficiency.

Japan's lifetime employment system then was not created arbitrarily on the strength of unique cultural traditions. Rather, it came about as Japanese companies sought to compensate for the wide differentials of technology and material capital that distanced them from their U.S. and European counterparts at the outset of the 1950s. It grew merely from rational behavior. What enabled lifetime employment to take hold was the sustained rapid economic growth that Japan enjoyed from 1955 until the first oil crisis. Had it not been for the continuous economic growth assured worldwide under Pax Americana, the Japanese economy would not have expanded as it did and it is unlikely that lifetime employment could have become firmly established. Companies cannot maintain the rigidity of employment and wages, as referred to in the Labor Ministry white paper, if the economy keeps slipping into negative real growth. Continuing economic expansion, although not the only condition, is an essential condition for lifetime employment.

On the other side of the coin, that same rigidity of employment and wages helped to sustain the high rate of economic growth. Japan's balance of international payments had been chronically in the red until the late 1960s. Net inflows of foreign currency declined as imports rose in an economy overheated by private sector investment in plant and equipment and other such stimuli. The government therefore tightened up the money supply in order to restrain demand for investment goods. However, consumer demand—kept strong by the rigidity of employment and wages—minimized the magnitude of economic downturns and facilitated recovery. This mutual dependence between lifetime employment and sustained growth formed a virtuous circle, which enabled the Japanese economy to expand at an average rate of better than 10% annually.

The union organization characteristic of Japanese industry is intimately linked with its system of lifetime employment. The company-based unions that are dominant in Japan today contrast with European and U.S. experience. Still, it is a mistake automatically to attribute them to traditional Japanese family culture.

Japan did not have a real labor law guaranteeing the right to organize until after World War II, but prior to this there had been a small labor movement. The labor union movement in Japan from the end of the 19th century through the 1920s was modeled on the European and U.S. pattern of organization by job or by industry. The labor movement reemerging after World War II did not feature company-based principles from the outset either. If anything, it again resembled the Western model.

Not until the 1960s did a large number of company-based unions appear. Impetus was apparently provided by the realization that a whole series of labor–management confrontations throughout the country, from the late 1940s to the mid-1950s, had brought only grief to both sides. Another possible catalyst was the growth of available labor. The market swelled rapidly as young labor shifted from agriculture to urban industry, with employee wages being set above the marginal productivity of farm labor. Considering that most of the workers in this new pool of labor acquired skills for the first time through intracompany training, it is hardly surprising that identification with the company should have preceded that with a particular job. Also, companies were growing rapidly right along with the nation's economy. This growth and the lifetime employment system drove real wages up remarkably between 1955 to 1974. There were few cases of serious labor–management confrontation at companies, and employees were seldom prompted to ask comrades at other companies to join them in going against their management.

The element of competition among companies in the domestic market cannot be ignored in any consideration of Japanese management and labor–management relations. And a survey conducted of its members by the union at one major coporation found that some 30% felt that fierce competition with other companies was keeping wages from rising as they should.

A Japanese company introducing a new product will ordinarily price it according to the competition, working beforehand to lower costs enough to allow for a profit at that price. This is classic price-taking in the literal sense of the word, as opposed to mark-up pricing—rarely used in Japan—in which margin is tacked on afterwards to costs incurred. Competitive pressure is thus the prime motivation for productivity improvement in the areas of quality and price.

Adam Smith identified competition as the basis for the free-market system. However, it must be remembered that companies had much smaller numbers of employees in that era and that competition among them was hardly different from that among individuals. With advanced technology, sophisticated capital equipment, and a huge corps of personnel, competition is a bit more complex. In economic terms, the individual has been replaced by the company as the unit of production activity. It is reasonable then to assume that the individuals associated with a company would want to cooperate.

The priority given to production teamwork at Japanese companies derives not from Japan's heritage of rice cultivation but from rational adaptation to the postwar economic environment. Japanese companies of the 1950s, poor in material capital and faced with the need to acquire technology from advanced Western nations, sought to minimize their capital costs. In order to produce equivalent products, they substituted labor for capital equipment, much of which was standardized in Europe and the U.S. Each company carried out this modification in its own way, resulting in gradually greater differences in the manufacturing processes used at respective companies for similar products. Employee training was adapted accordingly and inevitably reduced the interchangeability of workers among companies which reinforced the principle of lifetime employment.

If Japanese companies in the 1950s had lacked only advanced technology and the latest machinery and equipment but possessed ample capital, then Japanese management systems and labor–management relations would today be very different. Whatever else may be true of these systems, they certainly reflect the relative availability of Japanese resources at the outset of the nation's postwar economic development.

It should be clear that not only top management but all employees are involved in competition among companies in Japan. "Company loyalty" is not the point. This is all simply a matter of labor and management seeking to establish a reasonable working relationship; following the postwar period of mutually harmful confrontation, both sides recognize they are, after all, in the same boat. Unions therefore are not apt to make wage demands that ignore their company's competitive position, which has prevented the sort of wage–cost inflation seen in Europe and the U.S. For its part, management realizes that the company cannot compete effectively without the active cooperation of employees. It thus guarantees employment and pays the highest wages it can afford.

On the other hand, it is also true that attention to competition with rival companies has tended to weaken interest in the reduction of working hours. Be that as it may, however, criticism heard abroad that Japanese working hours are too long includes a great deal of misunderstanding and exaggeration. When one understands that the increased overtime put in by Japanese workers during periods of good performance is a safety mechanism for allowing companies to avoid layoffs during slack periods, it does not appear to be such a bad thing for labor. Members of Japanese management also point out that a reduction in working hours does not necessarily increase leisure time; it can actually lead to lower efficiency as workers take on second jobs.

At any rate, the respective interests of labor and management have been susceptible to conflict on grounds apart from intercompany competition since the time of Adam Smith. As a basic, free-market rule, working conditions must not be sacrificed in the name of competition. Labor unions must not lose sight of their responsibility for establishing and maintaining proper labor standards. Complex labor practices in every country have their own historical background. The industrialized nations need to exchange detailed information and carry out joint surveys and research in order to establish international labor standards based on unprejudiced, objective understanding.

PRODUCTIVITY AND THE ECONOMIC ENVIRONMENT

In the case of persistent economic stagnation, companies would engage in ever more vicious competition and do their best to raise labor productivity. Given stable demand, higher output per worker would reduce demand for labor. This arithmetic truth would make it impossible for any company to assure employment, and increased unemployment would be unavoidable. Reduced demand itself would obviously endanger the maintenance of lifetime employment, which would diminish the effectiveness of the host of management features usually enhanced by it. The scope of this discussion does not permit a detailed argument, but it is nonetheless clear that we must have continuing expansion of the overall world economy. The U.S. extended huge amounts of aid to Europe under the Marshall Plan after World War II and gave similar assistance to Japan. It also extended economic assistance to many newly industrializing countries. This aid stimulated the expansion of "effective demand" around the world, and thereby benefited the U.S. economy itself. The situation that J. M. Keynes warned of after World War I in "The Economic Consequences of the Peace" and that did in fact occur between the wars was thus avoided this time around.

Much of the criticism leveled at the Keynesians in recent years by the monetarists appears to be on the mark. Still, this does not impinge on the validity of Keynes' original "principle of effective demand." There is no reason to believe that Keynes, who was highly sensitive about the evils of inflation, would have disregarded the significance of the harmful effect of "inflationary expectations" as well as the kind of natural resource bottlenecks that caused the oil crises. But in the early 1970s, national economic policies began to recede. This was primarily due to mounting inflation, as the first oil crisis accelerated the pressure of wage costs in the U.S. and Europe and as governments introduced price indexing into fiscal policy.

Even more fundamental change was seen, however, as European and Japanese goods closed the gap on U.S. manufactures (and European agricultural products on U.S.), which had maintained undisputed competitive superiority in the international marketplace until around 1970. Countries shifted from the Bretton Woods format to floating exchange rates in order to accommodate the new circumstances, but doubt remains as to whether this was sufficient to deal with the closer competition among developed countries. The vast U.S. economic might served from the end of World War II through the 1960s to dispense effective demand around the world. This was the very key to the worldwide prosperity that made the world economy as a whole a closed system as presupposed in Keynes' theory. Accordingly, mere adjustment of currency exchange rates was not enough to cope with the new realities when Western European nations and Japan approached the U.S. in competitiveness.

Rather, what was needed was close cooperation among the U.S. and other members of the Organization for Economic Cooperation and Development (OECD). They needed to band together into some sort of organization for carrying on the worldwide task of creating effective demand, a responsibility which the U.S. had borne alone since the end of the war. The gap existing today between developing nations and free world developed countries is every bit as great as that which loomed between the U.S. and Europe/Japan in the late 1940s. The way to resolving the current global recession is manifestly clear. One need look no further to see this than the steel industry, where plant operating ratios are falling precipitously in the U.S., Europe and Japan—even as many regions in the world are in need of more steel. Good management alone cannot produce corporate vitality if the macroeconomic system is inefficient.

The Logic of
Japanese Enterprise

GENE GREGORY

Professor
Sophia University
Japan

A growing number of managers and government officials throughout the world are focusing their attention on the Japanese management system, partially in quest of an explanation for the competitive prowess of Japanese firms in world markets, but more recently with a view to discovering what aspects of the system might be adopted and employed to their own purposes.

Few would argue that the Japanese management system shapes the enterprise. On the contrary, experience and organizational theory teach that management systems are mainly behavioral manifestations contrived by enterprises to achieve their basic purposes. The enterprise, indeed, derives its reason for existence from the ability to adapt organization and methods to need. Essentially, it is an institutional response of those who control its destinies for their needs and those of society to manage advanced industrial technology. Management systems must be analyzed and understood in terms of the *enterprises* that fashion and use them, and these in turn in terms of the *societies* and the particular *individuals* whom they serve. Outside this context, the diverse elements of the Japanese or any other management system have little meaning or purpose.

In Japan, as in other industrial societies, the contemporary corporate enterprise is one of three main representative institutions, along with the family and the nation. Just as the family is the unique social institution for its special purposes and the nation state is sovereign in the realm of political order, the enterprise is the sole institution available to industrial man for the purposes of wealth. By and large, for their respective purposes the Japanese family and political institutions have served as successfully, if not so spectacularly, as the business enterprise. Yet the success of the former two has not generated the same enthusiasm abroad for learning from their experience as has that of the latter.

The essential differences between the Japanese and Western enterprises are at least as great as those of other representative institutions. The corporate enterprise as a legal device through which private business transactions of individuals may be carried on derives from different traditions and has undergone its own peculiar evolution, distinguishing it from that of Europe and North America. Organizational arrangements reflect familial patterns that are uniquely Japanese and are otherwise shaped by Japanese social organization and values.

The purposes of Japanese enterprise are defined quite differently from those of the modern U.S. and European corporation. The organic relationship between the enterprise and its essential members is quite unlike that prevailing in other industrial countries, as are those relationships that bind the enterprise to its external constituencies. As an organization of property, the Japanese enterprise resembles only superficially those in Western countries, where quite different traditional logic of property and methods of property tenure have played a determinant role in shaping the modern coporation. The notion that the enterprise is nothing but the property of its shareholders never gained wide currency in modern Japan.

However, the task is further complicated by the obvious fact that all Japanese enterprises are not alike. It is perfectly evident that Hitachi and Canon have little in common with the small maker of electronic components in a provincial city. In fact, there are in Japan, as in other countries, various kinds of business enterprise, all functioning within a common legal framework. Some are considered essential to the well-being of society; others are not so essential. Some are wholly subject to the vagaries of the marketplace; others are market leaders setting the pace of technological change and levels of prices in their respective sectors. It is also true, in Japan as elsewhere, that the image of the enterprise tends to be highly normative: it is what the enterprise *should* be. Deviations from the norm, in practice, are numerous and varied.

In this sense, at least, the Japanese enterprise is not unlike its Western counterpart. But there is considerably more consensus on both the character and purposes of the modern corporation in Japan than in most other industrial countries, which not only facilitates our inquiry but renders generalization more meaningful. To begin with, both reality and ideology permit us to proceed on the assumption that the corporate enterprise is an association of people, not an aggregation of assets. We can therefore identify three dimensions of the enterprise that will serve as a useful framework of analysis:

(1) the purposes and function of the enterprise as the key economic institution of the industrial system,

(2) the relation of the enterprise to its essential members and the ways in which its purposes and functions influence the internal management system, and

(3) the relation of the enterprise to society as a whole as well as to its other representative institutions.

Before examining these three dimensions it is important to understand the particular historical, economic, legal, and ideological setting in which they evolved and by which they were shaped. As the Japanese enterprise, like all social organizations, evolved as a human instrument for the purpose of optimizing a particular environment, its distinguishing traits were indelibly drawn by the reality that has been the context of its development.

THE SETTING OF ENTERPRISE

Business enterprise, wherever it is found, is essentially the logical organization of economic activity to obtain, as far as possible, maximum returns or product at minimum cost, under given circumstances. Returns may be not just monetary or material, but serve to promote education, health, amenity, or social order and harmony. Usually, however, the aim of those activities which business enterprise is uniquely equipped to manage is to obtain the maximum output, with maximum incremental additions to existing wealth, from given resources.

In this definition of business enterprise, the words "under given circumstances" are no idle embellishment. Different circumstances—rational response requires—yield divergent organizational structures and behavior. The penury of natural resources and the imperatives of technology transfer from abroad, for example, gave rise to the general trading company (*sōgō shōsha*) in Japan, and the scarcity of entrepreneurs in the early Meiji period, to the emergence of diversified industrial groups. It is, however, not just the availability or scarcity of natural resources or thrusting entrepreneurship that influence the form and performance of business enterprise, but also different historical contexts, geographical phenomena, market structures, imperatives of technological change, and financial requirements. Broader still than these variables are the types of societies to whose needs business enterprise must cater. Social organization, cultural values, educational levels, notions of property and laws, as well as political imperatives impose their indelible impressions on the purpose and system of cooperative activities for which business enterprise is constituted and managed.

In Japan, as in other industrial societies, modern technology has required the development of large-scale business enterprise, replacing the family as the representative economic organization. Large-scale business organization is, of course, the general condition of all modern industrial societies irrespective of cultural values and all the other relevant factors of the social system briefly accounted here. However, the character of that enterprise, which so pervasively affects the mode of living and destiny of the Japanese people, is not molded mainly by technology; what the Japanese want of it has been the decisive factor. What form of enterprise organization and mode of management best serves Japanese needs, rationally perceived or instinctively understood at a given time, has been the central concern of those involved in the cumulative process of its development. Purpose, which is the logical response to all relevant factors of the Japanese socioeconomic system, has been the underlying force determining the efficiency of cooperative action within the enterprise. And, since structure of business enterprise relates to purpose in a pattern of circular causation, organizational form as well as behavior are molded by this underlying objective and, in turn, determine the efficiency with which cooperative action pursues its attainment.

As it is just this efficiency of cooperative action that distinguishes the Japanese management system, this causal interaction of purpose, structure, and organizational efficiency is of central import. What deserves our attention here is not so much the efficiency of production or distribution of goods or services, as important as they may be for the success of business enterprise. Efficiency in the more fundamental sense of securing the necessary willingness for cooperative action by the individual members of the enterprise, which in the final analysis determines the vitality of the enterprise, is our main concern. Why Japanese enterprise has been more efficient in this sense defies quantitative analysis, but must instead be understood in terms of its basic purposes; and these purposes can be understood only in terms of the relevant factors to which they are a logical response. More precisely, the historical context in which the modern Japanese enterprise emerged, conspired with prevailing social, legal, and ideological norms to shape its basic purposes and behavioral patterns.

Historical Setting

The origins of modern enterprise in Japan were quite different from those of Western countries. Mercantile interests and bourgeois social norms played but a minor role in Japan's modernization at its inception. Although there were indeed a great number of commercial establishments in Tokugawa Japan (1600–1868), some of which still exist today, these merchant houses manifested little enthusiasm for the entrepreneurial opportunities of the industrial era introduced with the Meiji Restoration (1868). Traditionally, house rules had counseled against innovation, and their emphasis on practical business was not conducive to risky undertakings in industries with which they had no experience.

In stark contrast with the West, where aggressive merchants and bankers turned their capital to industry, becoming the architects of the large-scale industrial enterprise, in Japan the modern enterprise was fostered by public policy to develop a new breed of capitalist/entrepreneurs drawn largely from the former military class.[1] Industrialization was a matter of national survival, threatened by Western imperial powers, which had begun their encroachment by imposing extraterritorial authority over Japanese foreign trade.[2] Modern business organi-

---

[1]Johannes Hirschmeier and Tsunehiko Yui, *The Development of Japanese Business 1600–1980,* 2d ed., London: Allen & Unwin, 1981, pp. 95–103.

[2]G. C. Allen, *A Short Economic History of Modern Japan,* 4th ed., London: Macmillan, 1981, pp. 23–48.

zation found its chief justification in the conviction that building new industries was indispensable to assure the nation's political and economic independence, and that this could be achieved only by joint stock companies (*kabushiki kaisha*), which would enable the mobilization of capital and skills required to manage industrial technology.[3,4]

From its inception, Japanese enterprise was conceived primarily as a social institution with a national cause of the highest order: survival. Its principal promoters, men like Eiichi Shibusawa (1840–1931), Tomoatsu Godai (1834–1885), and Yukichi Fukuzawa (1835–1901), ex-samurai with their roots deep in Japan's agrarian past, were inspired by the conviction that a radical departure in both form and spirit from the commercial institutions of Tokugawa Japan was imperative if modern industry was to be developed and the fabric of the new social system woven with the woof of traditional ethical principles and the warp of modern technology. If they chose the European joint stock company as the most appropriate form for pooling capital for this common purpose, they drew heavily on the *Analects* of Confucius to attract and inspire a new breed of entrepreneur from the ranks of the disestablished samurai class and wealthy farmers for whom the practice of business was viewed with opprobrium.

> The company form of enterprise, Shibusawa believed, made it possible to entrust direction and management to capable and progressive men, whether or not they had capital of their own. While extolling vigorously the necessity of industrialization for sake of the nation, Shibusawa, like Fukuzawa, emphasized the need for education in the conduct of large-scale enterprise, elevating the development of Japan's human resources to one of its principal purposes. Moreover, for Shibusawa and his many followers, the common good, the progress of industry, was more important than personal gain and power, and they demonstrated this attitude in organizing and operating for years industrial undertakings from which they expected no immediate pecuniary returns. Stated succinctly, in the words of Tomoatsu Godai, the founding-father of modern Osaka business, "The wealth of the Empire must never be considered a private thing. . . . My hopes will be fulfilled when the happiness of the nation is secured."[5]

The historical coincidence of the crusade for industrialization to assure the survival of the nation and the emergence of the community-centered entrepreneur from the ranks of agrarian-based ex-samurai and wealthy farmers not only imbued early modern Japanese enterprise with social and economic purpose; it also

---

[3]M. Y. Yoshino, *Japan's Managerial System: Tradition and Innovation*, Cambridge, Mass.: The MIT Press, 1968, pp. 50–65.

[4]Companies, according to the Commercial Code of 1980, are of three kinds: *gōmei-kaisha* (commercial partnership), *gōshi-kaisha* (limited partnership), and *kabushiki-kaisha* (limited company). Most industrial firms in Japan are organized as *kabushiki-kaisha*.

[5]Byron K. Marshall, *Capitalism and Nationalism in Prewar Japan: The Ideology of the Business Elite, 1868–1941*, Stanford: Stanford University Press, 1967, p. 36.

assured its endowment with the hierarchical organizational patterns and cooperative management practices of familial ricefield agriculture. Just as the family was the organizational common denominator of premodern Japan, it became the unifying organizational principle of Meiji industrial society.

The necessity of rapid industrialization reinforced the pragmatic and ideological inclinations of the new breed of businessmen to draw heavily upon past modes of production, adapting them to the structural and organizational needs of industrial technology. Consistent with the rejection of economic individualism of the West and its emphasis on the profit motive, Meiji business leaders stressed the interdependence of men in society. In his discourse entitled ''An Explanation of the Harmony between Morality and Economics,'' Shibusawa argued that ''all sorts of industrial work and the existence of cooperative systems are conducted according to certain regulations based on moral reason and mutual confidence.''[6] The application of the traditional family system in the modern industrial context gave rise by the end of the Meiji era (1868–1912) to the embryonic forms for which the Japanese management system has since become reknowned: recruitment of company employees directly from school, lifetime employment, rewards based upon seniority, and a corporate welfare system. Moreover, as the family system became more institutionalized and intrinsically linked to the legal and political system of the period, the emotional appeal of industrial employment was enhanced for workers whose background was, in the main, in rural agricultural society.

Economic Setting

The sense of necessity and urgency that motivated the creation of the modern enterprise as an instrument for national survival was derived not only from the external political threat, but also from Japan's economic reality. Deprived of natural resources, industrialization was a precarious undertaking from the outset. Leaders of both government and business were acutely aware that Japan must import the technology and raw materials needed for modern industry, and that those imports as well as all other requisites of an industrial nation had to be obtained from the value added in production processes. In a word, survival depended on production; and the enterprise was the logical—ultimately the essential—organization for production.

It was clear to the promoters of Japanese enterprise that its essential purpose was to manage scarcities in such a way as to produce the most for the least. Waste of resources was to be avoided. Efficiency became a transcendental cause. Since the purpose of efficiency was not mainly to increase profits of the enter-

---

[6]*Ibid.*, pp. 38–39.

prise for the enrichment of shareholders, but rather to build a "rich nation and strong army" (*fukoku-kyōhei*), it became a principal management objective of the Confucian-inspired entrepreneur.[7] Efficiency was for the common good; and as it was in the national interest, it took preference over short-term profitability in the hierarchy of management objectives.

However, the logic of this perception was not just the understanding of management and government; it was a perception instilled in those working on the factory floor and in the man on the street. Indeed, every Japanese school child came to understand the compelling logic that, since Japan has no natural resources, the nation has to survive from the wealth it creates in production. Since national survival is at stake, it behooves one and all to do their utmost to maximize the creation of wealth. It is also generally understood that this is the basic purpose of business enterprise, and it is the shared experience that such purpose can best be attained through cooperative group effort.

From this basic reality of economic life, modern Japanese enterprise has, willy-nilly, derived its priorities. Nurturing cooperation for efficient and rapid growth in production became the first concern of management. Technology relating to these vital objectives was given highest priority. Training of managers and workers for effective cooperation commanded at least as high a priority as training in new skills. The system of finance had to be adjusted to these realities, and since these basic concerns could not be satisfied in the short-term, the inclination of managers to take the long-term view of enterprise objectives and their attainment was fortified.

As the political threat to Japan's survival subsided, the threat implicit in its economic reality was felt ever more acutely. Industry grew in size and complexity and the sense of dependence on the outside world increased. Key industries became increasingly reliant on foreign sources of supply and world markets, especially after the loss of overseas territories, the rapid industrial expansion of the postwar period, and the emergence of an affluent consumer society. As the threshold of wealth required for survival rose, the precariousness of Japan's economic security seemed to increase accordingly. Strong corporate enterprise capable of effectively managing far-flung international operations in an ever more complex environment became a sine qua non of national survival and continued economic growth. Survival was increasingly perceived as depending upon harmony and cooperation within the enterprise, as well as between the enterprise and other representative institutions. In sum, the strength of the Japanese nation became increasingly dependent upon the organizational efficiency of business enterprise. The challenge that gave rise to the Meiji entrepreneurs is as real in the 1980s as it was a century ago.

---

[7]Johannes Hirschmeier, *The Origins of Entrepreneurship in Meiji Japan*, Cambridge, Mass.: Harvard University Press, 1964, pp. 143–145.

Legal Setting

The distinguishing characteristic of the Japanese enterprise, then, is that from its creation in the 1880s it has been perceived as a social institution essential to national survival. Yet this vital economic institution, whose function is tantamount to being a public one, is *private* enterprise, and over the past century the Japanese government has consistently been intent on keeping it that way.

This being so, the question arises: Is the concept of "private enterprise" in Japan the same as in those countries where the institution first appeared? In Europe, business enterprise evolved as essentially private property, which was the objective of a vast and comprehensive body of laws in most countries. Since the Renaissance, and the commercial revolution that sustained it, the enterprise has been identified with its owners, who generally have been considered to have absolute rights of management and disposal assured in law. However, until the Meiji Restoration of 1868, Japan did not have a systematic and comprehensive body of commercial law. The laws in force before the Meiji era were a patchwork, largely derived from Chinese jurisprudence and Confucian inspiration. Designed mainly for the samurai class, they embodied and institutionalized the Confucian principles and feudal relationships that sustained the Tokugawa system. The object of law in Japan was not to establish or protect rights of any kind; rather, it was intended to maintain public order and assure the receipt of revenues on which that order depended.

Whether property held by individuals was "private" or "public" is indeed a moot point. Clearly, the distinction, if it can be said to have existed, was quite different from that of modern Western systems. In the older language, the term *ōyake* ("public") originally meant "the principal family," the Imperial House. Landholding by others entailed principally the duty to work the land to assure payment of the assessed taxes to the local administrative authorities, who, in turn, were responsible for their delivery to the overlord's warehouse. As this responsibility was nontransferable, land held by families identified in the surveys of the early Tokugawa period was inalienable, and thus could be neither bought nor sold. "Private" property was clearly "imbued" with "public" purpose.

In seeming departure from this principle, the private property system—based on principles of "modern ownership" introduced after the dawn of the Meiji era and taken largely from French and German legal codes—is characterized by the grant of rights "to control the property absolutely and exclusively." In practice, however, the notion of ownership held by Japanese is not one of absolute control. Agricultural land cannot be used for building, for example. Tenants cannot be evicted by an owner without due compensation: to insist on his rights would bring the owner public criticism and shame. Likewise, although as in other capitalist countries, a joint stock company in Japan is owned by its shareholders the shareholders do not intervene in management. Boards of directors, for the most part constituted from the top management of the company, consider them-selves to be *representatives of all the members of the enterprise,* not mainly the shareholders, and recognize an implicit responsibility to the public at large. Profit maximization, in the sense of the shareholders, is subordinate to the interests of the whole enterprise, its various members, and external constituen-cies.

Although the joint stock company was deliberately introduced to mobilize capital and attract professional managers needed by modern industry, it was in fact similar to its European model only formally. In positive law it was indeed "private property," but the social reality was something quite different. The modern Japanese enterprise was at its conception preeminently a social organiza-tion created expressly for public purpose, and legal rights of ownership were generally considered subordinate to that purpose. During its period of gestation and growth, the solidarity and strength of the enterprise as a social organization became a principal concern of both management and government policy makers.

Solution of social problems of industrial organization was instinctively sought in *culture* rather than *contract* as the basic reference point. As flexibility is inherent to the Japanese notion of law, changes in the social organization entailed no prolonged open contestation to seek legal satisfaction for social grievances. Changing social needs were met with adjustments in nonlegal social norms and practices applicable to the enterprise as a living social organization. It remained for interpretations of the law to adapt to the underlying social reality.

People in Japan, even judges and police, do not regard the law as determinant: the legal norm is expected to compromise with the reality of social life. Strict application and execution of law is regarded with disfavor as being unrealistic and too rigorous. As a result, lawyers play a much less important role in the conduct of all human affairs in general, and business in particular, than in Western countries. In all Japan there were only about 12,000 practicing lawyers in 1980, compared with some 500,000 in the United States. Legal departments are relatively insignificant in most Japanese companies and are not a recom-mended avenue to the ranks of top management. Furthermore, since lawyers are the defendants of contractual rights, their relative scarcity testifies to the lesser importance of contractual arrangements.

The Japanese have thus been less interested in changing the ownership of the means of production, the legal regime of private property imported from the West, than in construing the concept in practice to conform with Japanese social and economic reality and needs. Instinctively, the intent was to obtain all the advantages of private property while avoiding the disruptive effects construing property rights as being absolute. The construction given has been consistent with the character of the enterprise as a social organization and with its social objectives, assuring harmony within both the limited and broader social nexus.

The Role of Ideology

Ideology, rather than law, has been the primary instrument of social engineering in Japan. Traditionally, and especially in the Tokugawa era, Confucian ethics had played the central role of fashioning, legitimizing, and assuring participation in social institutions. Likewise, the Meiji leaders used Confucian ethical doctrines to introduce new modern institutions and to rally the nation to patriotic efforts through their instrumentality.

Modern business enterprise, perforce, had to be introduced into Japan within the context of the prevailing ideological framework. In keeping with the needs of the time, the new business ideology was called upon not to justify the private ownership of industry or to legitimize the authority of an existing managerial class, but instead to encourage private investment in industry and render enterprise management attractive to the educated classes, in particular the samurai *literati*.[8] It became necessary, therefore, to build new business institutions to manage modern industry, and to foster a new breed of entrepreneurs for this purpose. To meet this need, a new business ideology reflecting the cultural heritage and shared values of the samurai class was evoked by Meiji officials and elaborated by prominent business leaders and educators alike.

Accordingly, the major tenets of the Western capitalist creed were explicitly rejected in favor of traditional Confucian values. In particular, the Western prescriptions of economic individualism were roundly denounced for the stress placed on the profit motive; instead, a willingness to sacrifice for the common good and to nurture the nation's struggle for survival through productive enterprise was counseled. In brief, the task of the new ideology was to reconcile traditional community-centered values with the calculation inherent to the institution of modern private enterprise.

This new ideology was successful in elevating the status ascribed to men engaged in business activities. Those entrepreneurs who undertook major risks in launching new industries were especially the subjects of national acclaim. By the end of the Meiji era, the educated but somewhat hesitant samurai and wealthy farmers had developed into a new class of highly motivated entrepreneurs. The new business creed provided the philosophical foundations on which successive generations were to build. Equally important, however, the business ideology espoused by this new breed of enterpreneurs was eminently rational. Self-sacrifice made long-term economic sense at this early stage of industrialization, setting a pattern of a high rate of savings and reinvestment in new productive enterprise. This, in turn, had an important ripple effect, inspiring frugality and devotion to duty by others within and outside the enterprise. The substantial success of the new entrepreneurial class bore witness to the soundness of com-

---

[8]Hirschmeier and Yui, *op. cit.*

bining traditional values with modern technology, establishing the new ideology as an important feature of Japanese enterprise management.

With the rapid progress of industrialization, however, business leaders began to face problems of a different nature, which gave to this ideology a new role. By the early twentieth century, the main problem had shifted from one of creating a respectable image for business to that of finding an effective ideological rationale of the enterprise to assure the continued loyalty and cooperation of the growing industrial labor force. The increased size, organizational complexity, and bureaucratization of business enterprises tended to render impossible the traditional personalized relationships between employers and employees. Urbanization of the working class also brought important changes in social organization, which contributed to a weakening of traditional authoritarian hierarchical patterns of relationships, marked by a gradual replacement of the extended family structure with the nuclear family and the anomie characteristic of city life.

Remarkably, Japanese business leaders responded by turning to traditional family ideology for solutions to these new problems. By transforming the enterprise into a kind of extended family, a social reintegration was sought for all employees, managers as well as workers. Personnel practices adopted to give substance to this ideology were at once familial in nature and consistent with needs of the biological family of the employee. Permanent ties to the enterprise, advancement on the basis of length of service, and increasing attention to training were in keeping with the family tradition and actual family needs.

The new ideology, accompanied by the relevant personnel practices, enhanced managerial legitimacy in family-like harmony, unity, and solidarity, evoking strong personal ties and emotional attachment among members of the enterprise. Corporate philosophy peculiar to each company, but all embodying a common set of basic principles, became a standard attribute of Japanese enterprise in the 1920s and 1930s—and judging from the results, they were remarkably successful. So successful indeed that, after World War II, the new generation of professional managers gave new impetus to the established ideology by reinforcing and standardizing many of the familial aspects of the prewar management system. Companies gave added importance to the role of corporate philosophy, and business associations such as the *Keizai Doyukai* (Japan Economic Development Committee), established in 1946, undertook the formulation of a business ideology to meet the needs of postwar Japan. Once again ideology served to reduce tensions within the enterprise, to promote solidarity, and to establish a new harmonious relationship between shareholders, management, and the workers.

Management was deemed worthy to be entrusted with the stewardship of the enterprise, not only by the shareholders, but by the employees, suppliers, customers, and general public; it became a principal responsibility of management, therefore, to bring about a harmony of interests among the essential members of

the enterprise and its various constituencies. Corporate philosophies also generally affirmed that the responsibility of the enterprise went far beyond the search
for profit, stressing the vital importance of supplying products of highest quality
at the lowest possible prices through the most effective utilization of productive
resources to foster the welfare of the whole economy and the society at large.[9]

From the creation of the modern Japanese enterprise until the present, business ideology has been more pervasive, concerted, and consistent than in other
advanced industrial countries. Changing with the needs of the times, the prevailing business philosophy has successfully identified private enterprise with public
purpose, which in turn enables members of the enterprise to identify themselves
with it, secure in the knowledge that they are serving a larger purpose in their
work. It gives to that work a synergistic effect and, as a result, generates greater
personal satisfaction. Business ideology has effectively addressed the principal
problems of enterprise at the various stages of its development, providing a
perfectly plausible and wholly credible set of rational responses to vital needs.
People of the enterprise are not bound essentially by contract, but by a common
culture of which corporate philosophy is a vital part. Succinctly stated, shared
values make the business enterprise a human institution.

THE PURPOSE OF ENTERPRISE

The central problem of modern corporate enterprise in Japan, as elsewhere,
has been rooted in two basic sets of relationships: those between the purposes of
shareholders, managers, and workers, on the one hand, and between the purposes of the enterprise and those of society, on the other. Significantly, this
problem has been resolved quite differently in Japan, with far-reaching effects
not only for the enterprise management system but for the entire economy and
social order.

For shareholders, the intrinsic purpose of the modern corporation in most
countries where private enterprise has prevailed is to maximize profits, a purpose
that derives directly from their rights of ownership. Managers and workers,
however, being of average meanness, are not principally concerned with the
enrichment of others, but rather see the enterprise as an instrument for maximizing wages and salaries. The two purposes appear to be in perpetual conflict.
Traditionally, also, while the purpose of the firm as an autonomous business unit
has been to maximize the return on invested capital, the creation of wealth
through maximum production at lowest cost has been its primary purpose from
the point of view of society.

[9]Yoshino, *op. cit.*, pp. 95–117.

In Japan, profitability provided a convenient and useful measure of performance of the new enterprises and an inducement for the needed added investments. Yet, on the other hand, the profit motive was anathema to many of the leaders of government and business. Not only did it run counter to existing social beliefs of the times, but it was fraught with potential threats to the harmony of society as a whole and the enterprise in particular.

Fortuitously, the concept of harmony (*wa*) was foremost among traditional Japanese values.[10] Now the emergent industrial system threatened to destroy that order.

It seemed obvious to the new leaders of Japan that an industrial society based on private enterprise could function only if business contributed to social stability and the achievement of social aims. Yet profit maximization seemed inconsistent with the needs of the nation as well as the interests of those working within the enterprise. To attempt to justify the needs of business enterprise on these terms would not only do violence to the prevailing social values, but it would also invite conflict rather than harmony and thus slow the pace of industrialization considered to be a minimal requisite of survival. At the same time, it was important that there be no necessity or temptation to enact, in the name of prevailing social beliefs or national interest, punitive or restrictive measures inimical to the survival or strength of the economic institution on which the wealth, and ultimately the security, of the nation depended.

Two factors conspired, over time, to provide the needed unifying purpose of enterprise and its consistency with that of society: Japan's economic reality and family ideology.

The absence of natural resources, as noted, made it imperative for the Japanese to depend for their survival and development on the wealth they created in production. Immediately apparent, if Japan was to have industries, was the necessity to import raw materials, process them, and sell them in the marketplace for the best possible return. Resources therefore had to be concentrated in those industries that would assure maximum value added in production, thereby maximizing the wealth of the nation. Ultimately, this meant that individual enterprise had to be managed for maximum growth in output with the greatest economies of materials. By espousing the national cause through their business undertakings, the early entrepreneurs and their successors therefore opted for the maximization of wealth creation as their primary purpose.

---

[10]For centuries *wa* had been considered the ideal objective of social institutions and private comportment, serving as the central guiding principle of behavioral patterns within the family, community, and feudal system as a whole. Indeed, it had been elevated to the basic law of society as early as 610 A.D., when it was made the first article of the constitution promulgated by Prince Shotoku. Ever since, the harmony of society and its central institutions had served both as their principal means and purpose of existence; and the family, considered to be the natural harmonious order, had provided the principal organizational model for all other social institutions.

However, this purpose did not derive exclusively from the national interest. After the first signs of labor unrest in the early twentieth century, the reliance on family ideology to assure a more wholesome integration of the workers into industrial society added an important human factor. For lifelong employment and the rewards of seniority to be assured by companies, the necessary value had to be added in the production of goods and services to make that possible. Essentially, lifelong employment and the seniority system were designed to guarantee an equitable and socially consistent distribution of wealth, in keeping with human needs for security and integrity. For wealth distribution to be thus guaranteed, its creation had to become the foremost imperative of enterprise management. Moreover, if family ideology was to be meaningful, it became necessary to provide a measure of enterprise performance that would include the rewards to employees as well as those of the shareholders. Thus, added value, the wealth created in production, gradually gained general recognition as the appropriate measure of total enterprise performance.

It was not until the postwar period, when the needs of reconstruction and then of the Income-Doubling Plan introduced in 1960 forged this common purpose of public and enterprise policy into a formal instrument of management, that the concepts of wealth creation and added value became clearly defined. During this critical period, when national survival was again painfully at stake, industrial policy became necessarily more precise in its calculations of value added in production to assure the needed direction and pace of industrial structural change. Increasing concern with productivity required value-added accounting systems to evaluate output in terms of all the resources used in production. Revitalized labor unions required value-added statistics for wage negotiations to assure equitable salaries and working conditions; and financial institutions increasingly used value-added data in choice of investments and the assessment of risks. By 1970, therefore, there were nine different official and private value-added statistical services available in Japan to meet these varying requirements.[11]

Wealth Creation

Wealth creation is the essential economic purpose of all productive activity. A farmer generates wealth by growing crops and breeding animals, then selling them for more than the cost of seeds, fertilizer, foodstuffs, and other materials used. A retail store buys goods, stores them, displays them, and sells them. Thus

---

[11] Annual value-added statistics are reported by the Ministry of International Trade and Industry (MITI), the Ministry of Finance, the Bank of Japan, the Japan Productivity Center, and Mitsubishi Research Institute. These principal reporting services inform industrial, financial and monetary, fiscal, and labor policies as well as annual wage negotiations.

it adds value to the goods by providing a service for which customers are willing to pay. Similarly, a manufacturer adds value to the raw materials and components that are processed into finished products for sale in the marketplace for more than the cost of those materials and other purchases.

The amount of wealth created, then, is measured by the value added in production or the rendering of services. Simply stated, added value (*fuka-kachi*) is the difference between the sales revenue and the cost of materials used. In manufacturing, the margin between the price a firm can obtain for its products in the marketplace and what it pays for the raw materials and other supplies represents the wealth created, the added value.

Defining the purpose of enterprise as wealth creation, then, has the advantage of identifying its purpose with its essential economic function. Quite unlike profitability, added value has the decided utility of simplicity and clarity of connotation. Profits reported by companies may vary widely, depending only on the accounting practices used and differences of capital valuation. Moreover, profitability relates a relatively small part of the total output, the profit, to only one of the factors of production, the capital employed. Added value is a broader measure relating total output of all the factors of production and is therefore a more accurate index of enterprise performance.

In Japan, where the highest priority is placed on the efficient management of scarce resources, added value at the enterprise level becomes the more useful practical measure also because it defines the purposes of enterprise in terms of the continuing challenge of the Japanese economic reality—the creation of wealth through adding value to imported materials.

Some of the advantages of utilizing the value-added concept are:

(1) Since added-value accounting is far easier to understand than the conventional profit and loss account; it facilitates communication of accounting information to employees, showing them how they have benefited from the company's performance and enormously simplifying the task of explaining the need for profit as a reward to shareholders.

(2) Equally important, the added-value statement clearly shows the need for continuing savings and investments to generate more wealth in the future to be shared among employees, investors, and the other contributors to the success of the enterprise.

(3) Since profits are used only to reward shareholders, their main utility as a measure of performance is as an instrument for the management of capital. Added value, however, is the measure of the wealth generated by the collective effort of all those who work in an enterprise, as well as those who provide the capital, be they shareholders or lenders.

(4) Since before profits are paid to the shareholders, the government shares in the added value in the form of taxes, added-value accounting also serves as an

effective measure of the direct contribution of the enterprise to society and an instrument for determining the effects of taxes on the performance of the enterprise.

(5) Finally, since a portion of the added value is kept in the business as depreciation of tangible assets and as retained profits for reinvestment, added-value accounting becomes a more useful instrument for the management of investments than the profit and loss statement. Because added-value management covers a broader range of the company's activities, is reported in more widely understood terms, and makes wealth creation the central purpose of the enterprise, a wide range of critical variables command and obtain the full benefit of the company's managerial resources.

In practical day-to-day management, the concept of wealth creation and its added-value measure has wide utility. Since it provides a measure of output, added value can be used to measure manpower productivity in terms of how much wealth each employee generates. Comparison of this ratio between companies or industries also makes possible a determination of the relative effects of factors such as net tangible assets per employee on productivity. This in turn provides an appropriate measure of capital productivity.

As a communications device, added-value accounting resolves a wide range of problems, which otherwise are time consuming at best and often intractable. Since the purpose of the enterprise is presented in concrete, measurable terms both understood and accepted by employees and their labor unions, conflict between workers and managers in Japan has been noticeably reduced. Interdependence of labor and capital becomes immediately apparent, and the value of investment in innovation or new production capacity is rendered meaningful. The essential feature of Japanese industrial relations, then, is not that labor unions are docile, but that the purpose of the enterprise is defined in terms that are compatible with the workers' interests, and information about enterprise performance is readily available in terms that are both comprehensible and satisfying.

In practice, added-value accounting is used as a principal basis for annual wage and salary negotiations. Since the index of added value per employee and its allocation between contributors set a limit to the average wage per employee, it is the vital figure in these negotiations. No company can pay out more in wages per employee than a specified share of added value without influencing the rewards to other contributors or reducing the amount invested for future wealth creation, in which case all contributors will suffer in the future. In the process of negotiations, with all parties adequately informed, it becomes clear that the only way to raise real wages is to generate more wealth per person. The link between output and wages becomes patently obvious.

Yet these are not the only uses Japanese firms make of added-value accounting. It is also used as an effective tool of marketing and investment strategies.

In large diversified companies especially, concentration of resources on products with the highest ratio of added value to the limiting factors of production is critical if the firm is to maximize wealth generation with available resources. Moreover, since sometimes the same product may generate more added value if sold in different markets, added-value accounting becomes an important instrument of market selection and entry strategies. As strategic marketing is one of the more effective means of adding value to materials used in production, resource-efficiency conscious Japanese managers tend to be more responsive to market demand, which is the ultimate determinant of value. Management for wealth creation demands better products for better markets.

To meet this perpetually pressing imperative, added-value management serves Japanese companies as the bedrock of investment planning. Conventional capital expenditure practice in most free-enterprise countries estimates the expected profit from new equipment and the return on investment this assures. Although this calculation is made by Japanese companies as well, it cannot be the ultimate determinant of investment policy. Such calculations necessarily treat labor as a factor of production, a cost to be minimized and therefore only provisional. Since lifelong employment and the seniority system are the rule in Japan, the objective is necessarily not to maximize profit at the expense of wages but to maximize added value so that both wages and profits can be high. Thus, as wealth creation is made the central purpose of enterprise, people become the critical factor in the investment quotient.

In sum, as a measure of wealth creation, added value provides a set of business ratios relevant to all parties, the members of the enterprise as well as its customers, suppliers, and bankers. For the government, too, this is the critical ratio, not only because maximum value added provides a broader tax base, but also since the total value added by all enterprises in the country constitutes the gross national product on which the commonweal ultimately depends. In Japan, economic reality persistently hones public awareness that wealth must be created before it is distributed. The profit motive sustains no such popular wisdom.

The Technological Imperative

Value can be added in production in several ways, all of which entail either increase of sale revenues or economies of materials and services used in production.

- Higher total sales revenues can be obtained by expanding markets, but only by increasing the value of a given product to the consumer will it be possible to increase the revenue yielded by each unit of output. Consumers will pay more for improved design, quality, or function of a product, which in turn requires technological innovation.

- More efficient use of materials also can be readily obtained through improvements in product design, materials handling technology, and production techniques.
- Higher returns per employee or unit of capital can be obtained from these price differentials and materials savings by improved tools and production methods, which require continuing technological advance.

Increased wealth creation depends ultimately upon improved technology. It follows automatically and necessarily that the enterprises that adopt maximizing value added in production as their central purpose will ultimately succeed in effectively and efficiently managing technological advance.

The accent on wealth creation as the purpose of enterprise has six important consequences for the management of technology in Japanese companies:

1. To assure steady increases in value added through innovation, *Japanese firms give priority to production technology.* Although it is true that value is ultimately determined by consumers, the creation takes place in production. Recognizing this, outstanding engineers are attracted to the production line and they in turn have a strong voice in management. Many rise to top executive positions, and from their ranks emerge the chief executive officers of most manufacturing companies. This is vitally important for the maximization of added value. Since these engineers well understand the production line and the production process, they tend to give priority to investments for the improvement of production technology and to the more efficient use of scarce materials. This explains in large measure why Japanese companies have recently invested so heavily in factory automation.

2. As a result, *development, design, and production are closely integrated on the factory floor.* Research engineers are more likely to be found on the production line than in a laboratory distant from the scene of action. Of the 8000 or so researchers employed by Hitachi Ltd., to cite a usual example, only about 3000 work at the central laboratories. The remaining 5000 are located in the various factories and product divisions. However, some firms give even higher priority to the work place in their management of innovation: Nippon Electric Company (NEC), which employs 5000 technicians in R&D activities, keeps as many as 90% of them in the factories to assure effective communications and close cooperation between development and production. The result is a greater efficiency in innovation and a more finely tuned reallocation of resources to ever-increasing higher added-value products and processes.

3. Since value can be added in production through economies of materials and services, *R&D activities tend to give great importance to producing the best*

for the least. Materials conservation and new materials development are included among high priority national research projects funded or otherwise supported by MITI. Remarkable advances in energy-saving technologies throughout Japanese industry, although spurred by the successive oil crises, are also a reflection of long preoccupation with the efficient management of scarce materials. Likewise, Japanese leadership in fiber optics, carbon fibers, fine ceramics, and special metal alloys is a direct result of added-value management in new materials development.

4. Other major achievements of Japanese industry that have attracted much worldwide attention—miniaturization, quality control, and the *kanban* system of materials flow in production—are all directly determined by the diligent attention given to obtaining the best for the least. Miniaturization tends to enhance the value of products for consumers while reducing the cost of materials, and it opens completely new markets for new products with great economies of materials, thus enhancing the generation of wealth. Similarly, a principal reason that there are so few defects in Japanese products and that breakdowns are so rare is that Japanese companies consider quality control to be essentially a management technique for reducing the cost of scarce resources. The strong Japanese dislike of defective goods comes from the fastidious attention given the avoidance of waste, a practice that comes as second nature in a country marked by material scarcities. The same obsession led to the development of the *kanban* system developed by Toyota and used extensively at Canon as well as other leading Japanese manufacturers. By requiring suppliers to deliver parts and materials to the factory just at the time when they are needed for production, storage time and space are saved, reducing the net cost of materials in production. The result is higher added value or more competitive prices, and very likely both.

5. Since innovation is imperative for generating wealth in the interest of all members of the enterprise and society generally, *there is a remarkable absence of technophobia in Japan*. It is quite one thing for workers to be confronted with technological change to maximize profits for shareholders, often at the expense of jobs, and entirely another to know that the main result of those changes will be new opportunities for training, advancement, and higher wages. Moreover, as technology offers the greatest prospects for reducing the materials insecurity of Japan, it is widely regarded as having commanding social purpose.

6. Finally, the maximization of added value (and hence the creation of wealth) as the prime purpose of enterprise tends *to assure the availability of finances for innovation on terms and conditions most appropriate for its purposes*. Since interest on borrowed funds is paid from added value, banks are more likely to loan money to firms that attach highest priority to this objective and have a proven record of attainment. Moreover, they have a vested interest in providing capital to client firms to finance continuing R&D, as well as investments in plant and equipment, which are intended to increase added value in the

future. Thus Japanese firms are less dependent upon the vagaries of business fluctuations for financial resources to sustain continuing R&D than are their counterparts elsewhere. Since new product and production process innovation is often most important during recessionary periods, the availability of continuing bank financing for those purposes is vitally important to the process of wealth creation.

The net effect of defining the purpose of enterprise as wealth creation, then, is to make the management of technology, rather than the management of assets, its principal function. Technological virtuosity can become the goal of enterprise since its purpose is to generate wealth that is shared equitably by its members, and as the goal of enterprise it transforms management into high adventure in participative innovation.

PEOPLE AND ENTERPRISE

Modern Japanese enterprise was deliberately created in the Meiji era as an instrument of a society struggling for survival in the face of heavy political and economic odds. Organizational structure and behavior were closely identified with those of the entrepreneurial families. Employees, customers, and suppliers were not regarded as outsiders with whom the firm had no responsibilities other than to seek lawful contracts and bargains most advantageous to the owners, but were considered to be integral parts of the enterprise and its essential relationships.[12] These relationships, which remained in the natural rather than the legal order, were carefully nourished and preserved, passed on from generation to generation, as precious family treasures.

Thus, the prevailing reality of Japanese corporate life, common to all forms of economic activity, was its preeminently social character. As the spontaneous outcome of Japanese society's organizational formative principle, which for centuries had emphasized the family as the exclusive human nexus, the enterprise evolved as an organic formation of people rather than a creation of law. Legal institutions are generally imposed from the top down, decreed by elites with the expectation that they will engender at lower hierarchical levels the requisite motivational and institutional momentum. Such was the role of the promoters of the joint stock company as the appropriate form of Japan's modern business enterprise. Conversely, social organizations grow from bottom to top,

---

[12]It is remarkable, but generally overlooked, that suppliers of labor (employees) have essentially the same relationship to the Western enterprise as do other suppliers. In each case the relationship is contractual and at "arm's length." The employee no more regards himself as a member of the enterprise than do suppliers of other services.

deriving over time their inherent characteristics from the needs and aspirations of their constituent members. It was the needs of the migrants from rural areas who became Japan's new industrial workers, especially their need for identity and security in their adopted urban communities, which fashioned the character of industrial enterprise. A surrogate kinship relationship between company and employee became the basic social relationship in the city, substituting for the original extended family of which the migrant had been an integral part and through whose relationships he normally obtained a position in his new place of employment.

Nor was there anything unnatural or contrived about this transition. The traditional rural family (or, strictly speaking, the household) was never limited to blood relationship alone. The practice of adoption to strengthen or perpetuate the family was common and continues in modern Japanese society. Transferral of this practice to the industrial enterprise was both logical and in keeping with the natural order, providing an eminently reliable built-in recruitment and selection system. Employees tended not to be hired "off-the-street" from a labor market, to the extent that one existed at all. They were usually "adopted" at the beginning of their working lives either by *oyakata* (work gangs), which contracted labor to the enterprise, or by the enterprise itself through a more or less intricate set of personal relationships. Employment was not necessarily a contractual affair involving the performance of particular work or service, but became a kinship rite inducting a new member into the enterprise family to share in the work to be done.

It is in this very real sense that the Japanese enterprise is essentially people, not physical assets. Having been adopted into the enterprise family, usually upon completion of their formal education, employees—workers and managers alike—become members of the enterprise, not its hirelings.

Two basic features of Japanese enterprise, so constituted, have contributed to its organizational efficiency over the years. Most important is the consistency of purposes with those of its various members and, at the same time, with those of society. Wealth creation is at once human instinct and purpose, in tune with the needs of society. Wealth creation through the enterprise assures that the member's creative efforts are amplified in cooperation with others who share that common goal. Consistency of purpose fosters such cooperative modes of action, thereby optimizing the opportunities for synergistic attainments.

Consistency of purpose of the enterprise with its members and the other representative institutions of Japanese society—the family and the nation—assures a compatibility of organizational behavior that is mutually reinforcing rather than conflictual. The family, the enterprise, and the nation together constitute the basic wholly compatible organizational units of the Japanese industrial system, where the individual derives a most important attribute of his personality—his professional identity—from the firm in which he works. For the individual, membership in the enterprise is the vital link that situates him as a purposeful element of this system.

The Core Members

Employees are not the only members of the enterprise, however. As with all human organizations, the enterprise groups several essential members without which it would cease to exist. Game theorists have conveniently identified these players as the "core members." In baseball, for instance, nine players constitute the essential members without which a team cannot be fielded. A nuclear family requires at least a husband and wife, and if they are to be father and mother there must be at least one child.

For the modern enterprise, both people and money are critical, and since among the human contingent someone must take responsibility for various echelons of coordination and decision-making in the organization, it is necessary that some persons be classified as managers and some as workers. Shareholders, managers, and workers therefore constitute the essential or core members of the enterprise.

In most Western countries, the enterprise belongs to the shareholders, while workers and managers alike are related to it only by contract for the performance of certain specified tasks. By no stretch of the imagination can either managers or workers be considered "members" of the enterprise, nor would they admit to "belonging" to it. They only "work for" the company. In principle at least, all levels of the enterprise work for the enrichment of the shareholders, who are themselves anonymous and transient, but the maximization of profits, a goal that some managers may willingly adopt, is not one with which the ordinary worker, nature being what it is, can easily identify. The short-term gains of stockholders are seemingly incongruous with long-term vital interests in job security and pecuniary rewards in keeping with increasing family obligations. Moreover, the perceived identification of management with the pecuniary interests of the shareholders suggests to the wage-earner that the goals of enterprise to maximize profits are pursued mainly at his expense.

In stark contrast with this pattern of conflictual relationships in most Western firms, Japanese enterprise is distinguished for its cohesiveness and prevailing cooperative spirit. Unity and a perceived interdependence of its members are founded upon shared values and common purpose. Since the notion of the enterprise as property was never preponderant in Japan, and profits are subordinate to the superordinate goals of wealth creation and harmony, shareholders' rights do not take precedence. Since shareholders are transient as well as anonymous, they are neither viewed as belonging to the enterprise nor do they consider themselves as members of the enterprise. The permanent members of the enterprise, those actually working in it, are the active members with a real sense of belonging. Their rewards in the broad sense of the term, are accorded primacy of place among the claims on the wealth created in the business.

However, pecuniary compensation is not the main reward or motivation of the permanent members of the enterprise. Identification itself and development are more important considerations. Workers and managers alike identify themselves with the goals of the enterprise, and their most important identification is, reciprocally, the name of the company for which they work. They belong to the enterprise in the same sense they belong to a family and, as in the family, a living reciprocity of obligations and rewards binds them to the enterprise in common destiny. As they are strongly identified with as well as by the goals of enterprise, members are moved all the more strongly to try to improve it. Identification as the primary reward becomes the operative motivation. It is also the most personally reputable one.

Significantly, identification is shared more equally within the enterprise than are the pecuniary rewards. Managers are no more or less identified with the goals of the enterprise than are the workers. In the post-World War II period at least, management has not appeared to be in the service of ownership, but rather has been made responsible to all members of the enterprise and, indeed, to society generally.

The prime qualification of a Japanese manager is his acceptance by the work group; the group's harmony and spirit of cooperation sustain him in his role. Since managers usually move from one department of a firm to another in order to develop an acquaintance not only with the various activities of the firm but also with other members of the enterprise, they tend to strengthen the unity of purpose and sense of common identity within the entire company. Managers constitute a communications network within the enterprise, among the various work groups, rather than a top-down chain of command in the service of unknown shareholders.

In the context of Japanese enterprise, therefore, the usual labor vs. management dichotomy found in the West is notably absent. Since both workers and managers find their common identity in the enterprise and agree on its central purpose, the main concern of labor–management relations shifts from wages, salaries, and working conditions to assuring the necessary growth to secure lifelong employment for all permanent members and to sustain the seniority reward system. Since the workers have as great a stake in growth and wealth creation as management, they are organized into company unions. Not surprisingly, these company unions tend to resent the intrusion of labor federations in their affairs, especially when the interference is contrary to company interests. Instead, the company union finds it eminently more useful to join with management to foster security of employment and, to that end, the fullest development of the human resources of the enterprise.

Corporate Life Cycle

As with the family, the enterprise grows mainly through the development of its members. Increases in assets, production, sales, or market share are all indications of company growth, but they are the results of advances in human skills and the ability to employ them effectively in concert. To be enhanced, wealth creation entails technological improvement, and such innovation ultimately requires development of the people of the enterprise to produce better products for less.

Here the lifetime employment system finds its most compelling economic justification. For the enterprise to obtain full value in its investment in human resource development, training should begin early and continue throughout the employee's life. Optimal contributions of human resource development to wealth creation therefore entails, as a minimal requirement, a lifelong employment system. The central purpose of Japanese enterprise prescribes this essential condition.

What is involved in this process is clearly not just the development of specific skills, but the development of people in the fullest sense of the term. The two approaches obtain quite different results.

In Japanese companies, the training process begins with emphasis on preparing new recruits for a lifetime of purposeful cooperation with other members of the family. Human resource development involves first and foremost development of a sense of interdependence and a capacity for cooperation. Companies begin, appropriately enough, not with skill training but with emphasis on spiritual education (*seishin kyōiku*) to equip the initiated with spiritual power (*seishin-ryoku*) considered to be the key to good human relations. High priority is given to providing meaning to work beyond the task performed or the product it produces. Important, too, is understanding that the company is mainly concerned with the development of character, not the exploitation of human resources.[13] This does not mean, of course, that basic skills training is not important, but the more fundamental training is in company values, inculcated throughout the careers of each member and intensively instilled in each new recruit. The objective is to develop the total person through a comprehensive training program that includes skill development, physical fitness and health, spiritual values, social activities, recreation, and culture.

Once again, the principle of consistency fortifies the Japanese enterprise

---

[13]Specific examples of the role of spiritual education and character-building as a part of company training programs are described in depth in Thomas P. Rohlen, *For Harmony and Strength: Japanese White-Collar Organization in Anthropological Perspective*, Berkeley: University of California Press, 1974, pp. 192–211, and Richard Tanner Pascale and Anthony G. Athos, *The Art of Japanese Management*, London: Penguin Books, 1981, pp. 49–52.

system. Within the enterprise, training programs which stress development of the whole person strengthen identification of the individual with company purposes, providing motivation which transcends pecuniary compulsion. Perhaps even more important, however, is the consistency of this development process with human nature and the requisite of family life.

At the same time, the enterprise commitment to human resource development is consistent with national purpose. Since Japan's survival and growth are almost wholly dependent upon the quality of its human resources, for the enterprise and its members training is a fulfillment of a most important social responsibility. Only through continuing and extensive training programs can Japanese industry sustain the pace of structural change required by rapid technological advance and erratic gyrations of supply and demand in world markets.

ENTERPRISE AND SOCIETY

It has in recent years become fashionable to insist that Japan itself is like a corporation, with MITI as its headquarters and each enterprise a branch, division, or subsidiary of "Japan, Inc." The analogy, intended to describe the relationship between the enterprise and society in a word, in fact does more to confound the Japanese reality by describing it in terms of Western experience than to explain what it actually is. It is already apparent from our analysis here that the Japanese enterprise itself differs essentially from its Western counterpart. As people at work, the Japanese enterprise is an eminently human institution in which people are on top and money is on tap. It is not an organization essentially constituted of assets, nor can it be regarded strictly speaking as property; rather, it must be seen as a living organism that is not susceptible to being freely traded in an open "takeover" market, as is the Western corporation.

Just as the semantics and terms of reference used to describe the internal organization and behavior of the Western firm are often illy adapted to the analysis of the Japanese enterprise, so the notion of Japan, Inc., which has even less relevance to reality, adds little to our understanding of the relationship between Japanese enterprise and society in general, or between Japanese business and government in particular. This euphemistic term at best connotes an underlying consistency of Japanese social institutions, while consecrating illusions about the nature of relationships between them. It masks the consistency of purpose and the family organizational principle, which is common to all representative Japanese social organizations, with their implicit concern for equity and growth. It safeguards the illusion that MITI manages Japanese industry, as if it were one giant conglomerate, issuing directives for immediate compliance by private enterprise. To understand the actual underlying relationship between Japanese business and society and dispel this illusion, it is urgent to clarify the reality that the language of convenience obscures: private enterprise in Japan is a social organization, familial by nature, with an inherent public purpose, in the broadest sense of the term.

The matter strikes deep into the psyche of Japanese personality itself. Japanese do not believe that the public and private aspects of persons or institutions are separate in nature, but rather that nature requires them to be in fundamental harmony.[14] Since nature is viewed as a hierarchy proceeding from heaven to earth, from the higher to the lower order, precedence must be given to the public aspect to assure the intended harmony. This ascendancy of the public aspect has been further related in historical experience to an inherent "external" orientation of ethics and social values. Individuals, and all human institutions, acquire their value from outside, from society, from others, rather than internally. Men and human institutions have traditionally moved and been moved by their perception of what is expected of them.[15]

In keeping with these deeply ingrained social values, the role of modern corporate enterprise was inevitably distinguished and defined primarily in terms of its public role and function, rather than any particular private purpose or ambition involved. Although private profit seeking has existed and continues to exist in Japan, as it has in all societies in almost every age, the unabashed identification of public good with private gain as embodying the highest democratic ideal is antithetical to the prevailing ethos and therefore has been rejected as quite unsuitable, even barbarous. Rather, private enterprise has been expected to adopt and emphasize goals that are consistent not only with the vital interest of its core members, but also with those of the family, the nation, and the consuming public. In sum, the enterprise does not exist for itself alone, but is the vital economic link in a chain of related social institutions. Its purposes, therefore, are necessarily defined in terms of the chain, not the link itself.

Enterprise and Family

As the industrial enterprise came to replace the rural extended family, not only was its organization structured on traditional kinship lines, but the enterprise became in a very real sense a family of families. The employee did not contract to provide specific services to the firm, but rather became a member of an organic institution, whether that be the enterprise itself or an *oyakata* (work gangs whose

---

[14]Hirschmeier and Yui, *op. cit.*, pp. 50–52.

[15]The precedence given the public over the private aspects is closely related to an external orientation or formalism of ethics and social values. "Face" and etiquette tend to be taken more seriously, while recourse to one's private conscience is a luxury not recommended. *Ibid.*, p. 45. Also, see Hajime Nakamura, *Ways of Thinking of Eastern Peoples*, Honolulu: The University Press of Hawaii, 1964, pp. 409–413.

members were usually recruited from poor rural families by independent labor bosses), which engaged his total person, including his role in the family of which he was already a member. The enterprise eventually assumed full concern not just for the quality of work performance and skills, but for both the material and "spiritual" life of its employees, as well as that of their families. Each family represented in today's enterprise is encouraged to join extensively in its activities and benefits from company housing, welfare schemes, recreation facilities, cultural programs, and education.

Familialism as a foundation principle of industrial organization has required, as a basic condition, that enterprise purpose and mode of management be consistent with and supportive of those of the families of its members. Profits as an objective of enterprise are manifestly not an expression of family purpose, nor are they demonstrably calculated to benefit member families. On the contrary, there is an abiding suspicion, fortified by considerable literature, that the unbridled profit motive represents a potential threat to the families of employees, who will suffer if its quest is given primacy of place among enterprise priorities. The family has a readily recognizable vital stake, however, in increasing wealth creation by the enterprise: not only is the generation of wealth the only guarantee of secure employment, but its continuous increase creates the necessary means for family development and sustains the hope for higher standards of living. Indeed, lifelong employment, the seniority reward system, and the basic principle of equity in kinship-type organizations postulate the necessity of wealth creation's elevation to the primacy of enterprise purpose. Equity, security, and profits can grow concurrently only to a point; above this, threshold profits grow at the expense of equity and job security. Wealth creation suffers from no such contrariety.

The logic of familial organization and of the family support system has prescribed the organization and purposes of labor unions as well. Company labor unions are essentially a parallel organization of the enterprise family, which seeks to sustain its basic principles and objectives. The main role of unions has been to reinforce the lifelong employment and seniority systems and to strengthen company welfare programs, all of which are necessary to the interdependent development and strength of both the enterprise and its member families.

The motivational effects of this symbiosis of enterprise and family are obvious. The employee, having been born into the enterprise family at the beginning of his working life, identifies wholly with it and works as if he were working for himself and his family, not only for anonymous shareholders. Company loyalty comes as naturally and as intensely as loyalty to one's kinship group. The incidence of conflict between members of the enterprise family—between labor and management—tends to be reduced to the point that many companies can boast of never having had a strike.

This does not mean, of course, that all is sweetness and light within the enterprise, no more than family life is eternal heavenly bliss. There is disagreement, just as between husband and wife in a healthy marriage, but the underlying principle is that, like in the family, adjustments must be made, and these adjustments are made on the assumption that, when all is said and done, the members of the enterprise family will pull together.

Social responsibility of Japanese enterprise, then, begins with this consistency of purpose and compatibility of the enterprise and family. Strong enterprise and stronger families, mutually supportive, contribute ultimately to overall social stability and harmony.[16]

Enterprise and Nation

Common purpose and organizational principle, it follows, are the determinants of relationships between the enterprise and government in Japan. As in other industrial countries, the industrial enterprise was historically the creature of the modern state for the expressed purpose of managing industrial technology with all its commercial and financial ramifications to generate the wealth of the nation. Business is expected to maximize wealth in the national interest. It is precisely this expectation that has attracted the elite of Japanese universities to employment in Japanese enterprise over the years, and that explains in large measure the nature of its performance. The self-made entrepreneur, too, eventually undergoes a conversion from selfish profit-seeking to socially responsible entrepreneurship. The larger and more visible the enterprise becomes, the stronger are the pressure of opinion and the expectation that it comply with the broadly recognized exigencies of its public role.

This role, and the perception that economically the nation is a family of enterprises, defines the relationship between business and government. Given common purposes, cooperation is possible, desirable, and compelling on its own merit. The further notion of clear division of labor between government and business, each with its proper role, renders that cooperation effective. Government agencies, for all their authority, remain lean and intervene relatively less in business than in other industrial countries. Their role, mainly confined to setting goals, taking the initiative in the processes of industrial structural change, and supporting industry in the achievement of these goals, is generally seen by business as helpful rather than restrictive; the bureaucracy is considered to be competent and devoted to promoting the national interest. Reciprocally, bureaucrats concerned with industry, trade, and finance generally consider private enterprise as the necessary and appropriate instrument for assuring maximum and efficient attainment of national goals.

---

[16]Hirschmeier and Yui, *op. cit.*, pp. 219–220.

That this functional division of labor and cooperation between government and business is viewed as essential to the efficient management of scarce resources is quite clearly the distinguishing feature of Japanese industrial policy. The notable absence of an adversarial relationship between government and business to those who consider this the natural state of affairs may well seem tantamount to conspiracy or collusion and downright unfair. However, this view—which is at the root of extremist notions of Japan, Inc.—obscures perception of the underlying economic reality that informs Japanese business–government cooperation and the deep sense of shared purpose that makes that cooperation possible.

Industrial policy in Japan is simply and clearly intended to establish goals that maximize value added in industry by steadily, systematically, and selectively shifting resources within companies and among industries to ever higher levels of technology.[17] It is eminently rational, wholly predictable, and commonly agreed to be imperative. It entails not only the support of new growth industries but, especially in recent years, measures to expedite the often painful process of adjustment of declining industries. The survival and growth of corporate enterprise commands the participative partnership of business with government in the continuing process of industrial structural change.

Enterprise and the Consumer

But the enterprise commitment to society does not end there.

Value is ultimately determined not by the enterprise itself, but by the consumer in the marketplace; and the consumer is society. Thus, when Canon Chairman Dr. Takeshi Mitarai says that Canon's corporate purpose commits the company to striving for the very best in every product and activity and so contributing to society, he is not expressing a self-serving banality. The commitment to excellence is an essential feature of Canon's perceived public character. "It is," as Canon's chairman likes to put it, "the backbone of Canon's entire multinational corporate complex." In fact, this commitment to the customer has concrete positive effects on the company's performance.[18]

Members of the Canon family take pride in their work, and seek to perform each task responsibly, secure in the conviction that in so doing they are serving a larger social purpose. It inspires Canon engineers in the development of new and revolutionary technologies. These abilities are rightly regarded as Canon's chief assets. On them depend the reliability and value of Canon's products. Thanks to

---

[17]Organization for Economic Cooperation and Development, *The Industrial Policy of Japan,* Paris: OECD, 1972, pp. 11–31.

[18]"The Spirit of Canon," *Canon Chronicle,* No. 88, March 1979, pp. 4–5.

them, Canon cameras and business machines in some respects represent a world standard.

Similarly, at Matsushita Electric, a central feature of corporate purpose is the imperative of customer service. "Our social mission as a manufacturer is only realized when products reach, are used by, and satisfy the customer," Konosuke Matsushita insists. "It is therefore vital for an enterprise to have the quickest possible information on what the customer is asking for. We need to take the customer's skin temperature daily." Matsushita has long considered the purpose of the company he founded in these terms: "Profits should not be a reflection of corporate greed but a vote of confidence from society that what is offered by the firm is valued."[19] Reflecting the founder's ideas on how the firm should be run, executives at Matsushita give highest priority to customer satisfaction. "Our objective," Masaharu Matsushita told a visitor during his term as president, "is to serve the public by supplying products which help to improve living conditions."[20] There appears to be no doubt whatsoever at Matsushita that it is this approach that transformed the small electrical business, which began with the production of a simple double electric light adapter, into one of Japan's major industries. If this has been possible, he believes, it is because the company has provided its members with a meaningful way of linking their productive lines to society.

Thus, in a very real sense, the products of the enterprise become a symbol, not only of the skills and character of the people working in the company, but of their overall contribution to society; the value the customer places on those products becomes a meaningful measure of their performance.

Here again, consistency of purpose is the vital link. Customer satisfaction attaches higher value to the company's products, determining the wealth it generates for distribution to its members and constituents. With wealth creation the primary goal of enterprise, customer satisfaction becomes an absolute priority of business. Service to the customer is the best assurance of corporate survival and the critical factor in determining the rewards accruing to all members of the enterprise, not just to the shareholders in the form of profit. Since the value so created by all companies equals the gross product of the nation, customer satisfaction is, in a very real sense, the fulfillment of a fundamental social purpose of business enterprise.

---

[19]Rowland Gould, *The Matsushita Phenomenon*, Tokyo: Daimond-sha, 1970, p. 152f.

[20]David Oates, "Matsushita Electric Meets New Challenges," *International Management*, October 1974, pp. 24–28.

THE COOPERATIVE MODE OF MANAGEMENT

The significance of the above features that distinguish Japanese enterprise is found principally in their impact on the effectiveness and efficiency of cooperative management both within the enterprise itself and at the national level of the industrial system as a whole. The focus here is not so much on the productive efficiency of industry, as measured by the usual input–output ratios, but rather on factors that influence the capacity of business enterprise and other economic organizations to achieve their basic purposes. The effectiveness of any organization depends on the willingness of persons to contribute efforts to the cooperative system for which the organization is intended.

Admittedly, there is nothing novel in the observation that the effectiveness of cooperative activity within an organization is determined by the extent to which that cooperative effort furthers the interests of its members. Indeed, it would not deserve mention here but for the fact that business enterprise in most industrial countries is just about the only organization that is constituted in defiance of this fundamental rule. Farm organizations are expected to strive for legislation favorable to all their members; cartels are expected to strive for higher prices for participating firms; the state is expected to further the common interests of its citizens; while the corporation is expected to further the interests of its stockholders. Yet, quite clearly, the stockholders do not constitute the total necessary membership on which the cooperative efficiency of the organization depends, nor do the other essential members share a common interest with the holders of stock in the profits of the firm.

Much of modern scientific management is intended to overcome this basic fault, without fundamentally altering the organizational purpose of business enterprise. The inculcation of belief in the real existence of a common purpose among shareholders, managers, workers, and society is an essential, but practically impossible, executive function of most enterprises. The unhappy result has been a preponderance of persons manifesting a negative willingness to cooperate effectively for the organizational purpose of the enterprise. Instead, the general pattern in Western countries has been for workers, and even managers, to organize external unions in an attempt to alter the efficiency of the organization in terms of their various individual motives. Conflict has replaced cooperation as the prevailing mode of management. Of the possible contributors, only a small minority have a positive willingness to cooperate, with an inevitably deleterious effect upon the enterprise.

This state of affairs stands in stark contrast to the cooperative mode of management practiced by Japanese enterprise. Japanese enterprises define their objectives in terms of the interests of not only all the core members, but also external constituencies such as consumers, suppliers, and the government. The identification of this common purpose and the existence of persons prepared to contribute to the realization of such a common purpose are the two poles of the system of cooperative effort within the Japanese enterprise. The task of management is to transform this potentiality into dynamic action through effective communications. In fact, the task of Japanese executives can be stated simply as the *management of cooperation through effective communications.*

Communications and learning, in the final analysis, depend upon the attitudes and receptivity of the receiver and not the power of the transmitter, of the learner and not the teacher. The verbal communication of corporate philosophies and policies is essential, but much more important are the actions of managers and the enterprise which create the appropriate atmosphere for relatively static-free reception. Observational feeling, which is sensitized and informed through training programs and socialization of each member of the enterprise, is a most important aspect of this communication.

Communications techniques go far toward shaping the form and effectiveness of the organization. Offices in Japanese companies are typically open spaces, with everyone working physically together; in such an environment nonverbal communications tend to be more effective than in companies where everyone is enclosed in private offices. The common uniform worn by company staff members tends to remove barriers to communications within the firm, symbolizing that all—managers and workers alike—are *sha-in,* that is, members of the firm. Together they are collaborators working for the success of the enterprise.

Company unions are essentially an institutionalized communications channel designed for the instruction of managers as well as workers. Great care is given formal selection, training, and development of executives for their ability to communicate and inspire cooperative action. An executive's communications skills are systematically developed through cultural conditioning, specific training, and organizational experience throughout his lifetime in the enterprise.

The Japanese enterprise also comes equipped with numerous other important informal communications channels. Each class of new recruits establishes close personal ties that facilitate communications across formal organizational units of a company over the years of their membership. Close *sempai–kōhai* (senior–junior) relationships are established to serve as a learning mechanism that transmits the ways (*kafū*) of the enterprise from one generation of members to another. Socializing after office hours serves as a most important two-way communications system for transmitting information, the flow of which may be inhibited through normal channels. Sports and outings involving company members also play a role in the intricate network of enterprise communications.

Into this network is a built-in feedback mechanism on which all members rely heavily for their information about the company. If Japanese are generally much better informed about their enterprise, it is not only because they are lifetime members rather than contractual employees, or that they identify personally and wholly with the enterprise, but also because company organization and systems are devised and used to inform their understanding. Employees therefore implicitly regard their day-to-day corporate experience as a learning laboratory from which they acquire the wisdom and habits required for effective cooperative activity. Outside training, especially in business schools, has little part in this process and indeed is regarded as counterproductive for the instruction of effective cooperation.

> Significantly, "leadership" is not a word in the vocabulary of this mode of cooperative management; and indeed the Japanese language does not have a specific term for it. Like the father, the Japanese manager usually gets to his position not by recruitment from outside the corporate family through a "headhunter", but because he has slowly grown with the family, risen in the organization much as a father does. A very large element in his experience, training and continuity of association is the ability to understand with feeling, without reliance on verbal communications, not merely the situation or conditions of the people with whom he works, but their expectations and intentions.[21]

This attention given to effective communications techniques in the promotion of cooperation would not be complete, however, without a ready measure of the effectiveness of cooperative activity in attaining the purposes of the enterprise. For this purpose, the standard profit and loss accounting system is of little value, for it measures enterprise performance only in terms of one of the essential participants. Instead, it is the role of value-added accounting and data reporting systems to inform workers, labor unions, banks, and tax officials of the wealth created by the enterprise, as well as its competitors, the industry as a whole, and other industries—at home and abroad. Equally important, the information these reporting systems provide on the distribution of wealth created informs all parties concerned, in uncomplicated terms, of the efficiency of the enterprise relative to the rewards accruing to all the various contributors to the cooperative system. One of the specific purposes of these value-added monitoring systems is to secure for the enterprise all the necessary contributions required for its continued growth.

Such information has particular import for the management of cooperation between business and government. Since there is common accord on the purposes of economic activity at the enterprise and national levels, both being served by maximal value added in production, the necessary cooperation between enterprise and government is largely determined by the efficiency of communications. An intricate network of trade associations, deliberative and advisory councils, cooperative research associations, and personal relationships has been developed for that purpose. The flow of information is abetted as much

---

[21]Chie Nakane, *Japanese Society*, London: Penguin Books, 1973, p. 75.

by the compatibility of all these institutions as by the consistency of their organizational principle and purpose that motivates their members.

Material inducements for the individual members of the enterprise are effective only to a limited degree; monetary rewards do not contribute sufficiently to the cooperative system within the enterprise to enable it to be efficient to the degree necessary for survival and growth in the long run. To maintain an organization that lends prestige to and secures the loyalty of desirable persons is one of the main determinants of organizational efficiency. This entails conditions under which the pride of production through cooperative effort can be shared equitably by all members of the enterprise. The familial principle of organization provides the unwritten rules that assure such equity of intangible rewards and the satisfaction that comes from personal fulfillment. This cooperative system is further fortified by the continued imperatives of managing scarce resources and by the lingering legacy of Confucian values, with their emphasis on harmony and the public respect of the human personality.

These essential conditions for efficient and effective cooperative activity are thus assured in Japan. Common purposes incite cooperation because they are accepted by all those whose efforts are essential to the representative institutions at various levels of economic activity.

The Quality Control Circle:
The Komatsu Experience

RYOICHI KAWAI

Chairman
Komatsu Ltd.
Japan

Komatsu has constructed a management by policy approach in order to attain the company's objectives. Quality control (QC) circle activities are conducted as a part of this system and are carried out by the staff in the form not of individual but of group activities. The implementation of management by policy throughout the company was born in the process of introducing and promoting total quality control (TQC). The history of TQC in Komatsu will provide a background for the small-group QC circle activities.

HISTORY OF TQC AT KOMATSU

The production of bulldozers began to expand rapidly in the latter half of the 1950s, the period in which bulldozers were sold as fast as they were being produced. Following the liberalization of foreign trade and capital, the world's largest construction machinery manufacturer decided to form a joint venture company with a large Japanese enterprise leading us to experience a period marked by crises.

The quality of our products during that period was only half that of the international standard in terms of durability. The rapid upgrading of quality standards was the priority task that had to be promoted, as it was the only way Komatsu could survive. The quality improvement activity was termed the "circle A project," from the ace in a deck of playing cards, and was given the highest priority within the company. TQC was then introduced in 1961 as the instrument to ensure the success of the circle A project.

The president at that time ordered the staff to ignore the costs required to produce world standard products and to disregard the Japanese Industrial Standards (JIS), aiming instead at even more stringent quality requirements. The product created under the circle A project was called vehicle A, which was introduced to the market two years later. Due to this upgrading activity, the durability of vehicle A was increased twofold, and consequently the guarantee period was extended twofold. In addition, the number of claims by customers fell to one third the level we had experienced previously, indicating the great success of the quality improvement activity. Furthermore, the domestic market share for our products was increased from 50 to 60% and there was a further expansion of exports.

The product quality improvement activities have achieved their objectives and at the same time enhanced the quality of work within the company. The crisis atmosphere that prevailed when the vehicle A project was launched resulted in a spirit of unity between the management and staff that lasted throughout the project. It was the most valuable achievement gained from this promotional activity.

Circle A was aimed at the promotion of quality improvements for medium- and small-sized bulldozers. As the domestic market became sluggish following the U.S. monetary crisis in 1971, we strived for an expansion of large-sized bulldozer exports. Accordingly, the circle B project was implemented as the quality improvement activity for large-sized bulldozers following the success of circle A.

Both circles A and B were activities to improve product quality. We normally initiate such activities with a program of market research in accordance with the principles of TQC, the understanding of user requirements being the fundamental element in TQC. For example, in the case of the circle B project, we carried out market research by examining data on marketability based upon the actual results for 700 vehicles covering a range of domestic and foreign competing models, including our own bulldozers. The opinions held by users and servicing staff in representative offices were collected simultaneously. Based on the outcome of the market research, the target for quality standards was set, and development, production, sales, and after-sales services were undertaken accordingly. The promotion of this activity involved not only the staff in the design, manufacturing, and inspection departments, which are directly related to the products but also the staff in the administration, production technology, and material departments, which support the other departments. In other words, the whole company participated in the activity, working toward the common goal.

CONSISTENT POLICIES IN TQC

Through the implementation of the circle A and circle B projects, the entire staff has raised its consciousness drastically. To obtain such results a company should set a target, introduce TQC, and fully utilize the rules of TQC to attain the goal.

The basic concept behind TQC is continuously to repeat the managerial cycle "P (Plan) D (Do) C (Check) A (Act)," that is, to assess user requirements accurately through market research, weave the assessment into the target set for quality standards, compare the results in practice with the original plan, and feed back the reasons for any disparities observed between projected and actual results and provide for incorporation in subsequent plans. This concept is applicable not only to quality improvements, but also to cost reductions, delivery control, and stock control, and further to the broad range of managerial objectives. Not only factory production centers but also administration and sales/after-sales service sectors can benefit from the TQC concept.

A company must always be innovative; to this end, the basic policy and specifics of a target must be clarified so that all the staff members can fully understand what the company is aiming for in a specific time period. This is referred to as "management by policy" at Komatsu.

Setting forth a long-term management plan is the most important step to be taken for policy control. Komatsu always follows a long-term management plan encompassing a five-year period, which is enhanced by the so-called rolling system, whereby the project is reviewed between April and September of every year. In the rolling system process, the Corporate Planning Department is designated the secretariat for the project, where each headquarters and administration department of the head office analyzes and reviews the project in order to hammer out policies. As a result, the specifics of a target will be finally decided. The long-term management plan therefore has a target that is supported by every possible policy required to attain its materialization. After the long-term project is finalized at the end of September, the presidential policies and targets will be concluded in November. The policies adopted by each general manager, factory manager, and department manager are decided accordingly, and hence the activity program at each unit of these various sections. The preparation of plans is completed by the end of the year and they are implemented simultaneously when the new year arrives.

It is necessary to promote an understanding among all the staff of the policies selected by the president or factory manager. QC circle activities are integrated in the system of management by policy and activated at the base of the company's structure. They are carried out in such a way as to give the staff members an awareness of their involvement in managerial activities. In particular, the objective of a QC circle is to take part of the responsibility for the target of each section and to fulfill its share of the target through QC circle activities. The members of the QC circle are therefore aware of the extent to which the achievement of their objectives will contribute to the results of their department and also to the business of the company as a whole.

QC CIRCLE ACTIVITIES

According to the outline compiled by the QC Circle Headquarters in Japan, a QC circle is a small group that independently undertakes quality control activities within the workshop. As an element of the quality control activities carried on throughout the company, the small-group activities enjoy the participation of all the staff as a means of achieving successive improvements.

Japan's QC circle activities were initiated in 1962 by their advocate Kaoru Ishikawa. Komatsu introduced QC circles in 1963 and they are still quite active today. First the foremen received QC education in order to resolve problems related to the workshop independently. At the next stage, circle activities led by a foreman began within each of the workshop units. The activities were further diversified to each group within a unit, led by a group leader junior to the foreman. At present, the activities have been further refined with the creation of smaller groups with a leader selected from among the workers.

ORGANIZATION OF QC CIRCLE ACTIVITIES

To conduct QC circle activities with the participation of all the staff, Komatsu organizes the QC Circle Promoters Liaison Conference. The Quality Assurance Department has taken reponsibility as secretariat of the conference. Each headquarters and operating division stages its own QC circle promoters' conference, each of which is under the guidance of the TQC Promotion Secretariat. These secretariats produce an introductory reference for successful QC circle activities to encourage all the members of the circles.

EXAMPLE OF QC CIRCLE ACTIVITIES

How is a QC circle operated? What do the activities actually involve? Who will participate in the activities and what form will this participation take? Who will give guidance for the activities, and when and how? To answer all these questions, the following situation can serve as an example.

An affiliated company of Komatsu manufactures wheel loaders. At this factory there is an example of small-circle activities conducted by four female telephone operators in the factory.

Complaints were received one day from outside callers regarding delays in answering the telephone, which resulted in the operators raising the issue of effective telephone operating work.

In order to appraise the existing situation, they carried out a survey by distributing questionnaires among the staff asking what they expected the operators to do to improve the service. The results indicated that 102 out of the 150 surveyed (68% of the staff) expressed their dissatisfaction with the service complaining that the operators did not pick up the telephone quickly enough. Having ascertained that the complaints from outside were reasonable, the operators immediately decided to tackle the problem of improving their service. The theme they selected for this assignment was "the no-waiting switchboard."

As the next step, the operators recorded the number of incoming calls per day and the time required to answer each, with the following results: of the 811 calls a day, 62% required 5 seconds (the time taken by two rings of the bell, which is rather quick), 14% required 6–10 seconds (the time taken by three to four rings), and 24% required more than 11 seconds (the time taken by more than five rings, which may annoy the caller). On average, 7.4 seconds is necessary to answer one telephone call. Having discovered that the standard set by the Nippon Telegraph and Telephone Public Corporation is 3 seconds on the average, the members of the circle discussed how to improve their work to achieve the target of 3 seconds.

The results of the factor analysis using a property chart suggested the following measures to improve each factor. To alleviate peak period bottlenecks when calls were concentrated at specific times of the day, the handling of incoming calls could be shortened by omitting the step of informing the staff of the caller's name. To reduce the time spent looking for visitors, the name and location of these visitors could be communicated to the operators by a gate keeper. To locate the appropriate person to whom to address an inquiry, a chart showing job descriptions and names was prepared. Not knowing the locations of telephones, the operators were sometimes unable to transfer a line to a nearby telephone when the original line was engaged. A telephone distribution chart of the factory shortened this transfer time.

These measures resulted in a reduction of the time spent answering an incoming call to 4.7 seconds. Further, they checked the sections that tended to be slow in picking up the telephone and also telephones that worked slower than usual. As these sections became cooperative in answering calls, the group succeeded in achieving the 3-second level.

Through this process, the operators have learned to think about problems, elaborate a plan, express their own opinions, and cooperate with each other.

The QC circle assists the creation of good human relations and helps engender a feeling of satisfaction with the work by sharing the satisfaction of achieving a goal. People learn to work with their brains as well as with physical strength, but certain tools are necessary to facilitate an intelligent approach.

METHODOLOGY OF QC CIRCLE ACTIVITIES

Staff undertaking QC circle activities are instructed to equip themselves with seven tools, thoroughly explained in a QC handbook. The methods of applying these tools are taught through a group education program. Foremen and group leaders also help the staff understand the application of these tools to routine work. In the case of the telephone operator survey, the knowledge to compile a pareto chart and the factor analysis helped to solve the problem.

Familiarity with such tools to solve problems scientifically is acquired through thorough training. QC education has been implemented by the Komatsu staff in accordance with seniority, from top management to general workers.

ROLES WITHIN QC CIRCLE ACTIVITIES

Choosing a theme is the first difficulty encountered in starting QC circle activities. A theme emerges from an awareness of a problem. Discovery of work-related problems can best be made by workers themselves, but advice is helpful in the early stages. Taking the example of the telephone operators once again, the problem of delays in their answering calls emerged from their day-to-day work and was therefore a useful theme for the operators to tackle. If assigned the theme ''What is the most appropriate number of telephones in the factory''? they would not have had the capacity to handle it. Assistance in choosing a theme or advice on how to choose a base gets the activities off to a good start; follow-through advice helps ensure the project is carried out smoothly.

Another role is to create the best environment for the activities. When a discussion is required, a meeting room, tables, chairs, and a blackboard should be available, and the time required must also be approved. Komatsu has allocated two hours per month for QC activities to each member of the staff. Initially the staff carried out the activities within the given time period. However, once the satisfaction of attaining the goal of resolving a problem is experienced, the tendency to disregard the passing of time develops. When results are seen, however, the staff often holds meetings during their lunch break and after office hours.

PRESENTATION OF RESULTS

Once a QC circle has achieved an objective, it is important for members to summarize the activity results and to make a presentation. The telephone operators group leader wrote a report and the group made a presentation at the departmental QC circle meeting. They then participated at the factory meeting, their QC activity won first prize, and they obtained the right to participate in the All-Komatsu QC Circle Assembly held annually at the head office during November, the quality month. With this encouragement, presenters are able to develop their activities further through the experience of compiling the report on their activities.

We have set up a system by which everybody can make a presentation at any occasion; at the top of the system is the All-Komatsu QC Circle Assembly. To participate a circle has to win first prize in the sectional, departmental, and factory meetings consecutively. The qualification to participate in the competition is rigorous but carries a great deal of prestige within the company. The competition is authoritative, with the president attending and the executive director presiding as a judge. Winning a prize in this competition therefore signifies a high level of achievement.

FAIR EVALUATION

To summarize activity results for presentation and to win a prize is one of the ways to receive a high evaluation. Another way to evaluate activities is to check routine work closely; this is the key to encouraging staff to maintain their momentum. The company has adopted three methods of evaluating routine work:

(1) When a goal is attained, the report is prepared within one month and submitted to the secretariat of the operating division. The submitted reports are rewarded by a manager of each department within one month.

(2) As a semiannual QC circle award, a superior circle is rewarded by a factory manager who evaluates the number of themes attained and the meetings held using a marking system.

(3) There is a diagnosis of QC circle activities. Each circle carries out a diagnosis of their activities twice a year; based on the diagnosis, a supervisor interviews the leader of a circle to discuss progress and to present problems and guidelines for future activities.

From our experience, the extent of a supervisor's attention to QC circle activities determines the managerial standard in the workshop. A workshop assisted by a less than enthusiastic supervisor tends to have an inactive QC circle, the quality of work deteriorates.

ROLES PLAYED BY MANAGEMENT

The participation in the All-Komatsu QC Circle Assembly is open not only to representatives of Komatsu but also to members of affiliated companies, collaborating companies, and dealers, who are eligible to win a prize. The participation of senior members of the company has had a great impact upon the promotion of QC circle activities. The head of each operating division places importance on QC circle activities, encouraging members of his group to win a prize. The head of each operating division and the supervisors consequently have no choice but to concentrate their energy on the activities. Although QC circle activities are known as independent activities, they will not continue to grow unless top management and supervisors indicate their interest through consistent and concrete actions.

THE OFFSHORE UNIVERSITY

The All-Komatsu QC Circle Competition is staged at three venues annually and a gold prize winner is selected at each. As a reward, these three contestants are dispatched to the QC Circle Offshore University (a passenger vessel) organized by the Union of Japanese Scientists and Engineers. During the two-week cruise the representatives participate in seminars and discussions, where they exchange their opinions with leaders representing other companies throughout the country. Leaders return with an enriched personality and broader vision, and take an active part in promoting QC circle activities in their own operating divisions.

QC CIRCLES UPGRADE OF PERSONNEL

QC circle leaders are neither group leaders nor foremen but normally are appointed by a group leader, who bases the choice on staff members' work and leadership potential. A new leader usually faces many difficulties managing circle activities. With advice, however, the leader learns to manage the circle even if through a series of failures and disappointments. Self-confidence and leadership ability gradually develop to provide the stimulus to tackle the next theme. Through such experiences, a QC circle leader develops into a capable staff member and is normally promoted to group leader. QC circle activities therefore create the best environment to create the supervisors of the next generation.

CONCLUSION

There is the satisfaction of achievement in work, and of cooperating with a colleague and having the approval of others. A member must be aware that he has his own role to play in QC circle activities and in helping other members feel job satisfaction, in addition to his contribution to the achievement of the company's objectives. It is characteristic of Japanese companies that the feeling of achievement obtained through the activities is shared among the group rather than concentrated on the individual. On a personal level, though, there is the self-satisfaction of witnessing growing maturity and feeling enrichment in life.

The QC circle has proven to be a successful method for employees—as both individuals and a group—to realize satisfaction through their work.

As long as such activities continue, the vitality of the company will never be lost. The world economic recession has given rise to many problems. The revitalization of the economy must begin in each company, which should be capable of undertaking a vital activity, for otherwise the whole economy will never regain its vitality.

Quality-Sustaining Competitiveness in the Japanese Auto Industry

TAKASHI ISHIHARA

President
Nissan Motor Co., Ltd.
Japan

Quality can be improved most effectively when firms are stimulated by competition. Competitiveness is the basic motivating power that promotes vitality in individual corporations and in industry in general. Several conditions are necessary to ensure the vitality and growth of a corporation. First, the environment both within and surrounding the firm must be supportive of business vitality. More specifically, the political, economic, and social environment must be conducive to the healthy functioning of the market mechanism under the principle of free competition. Equally vital to a healthy market mechanism are certain cooperative interfirm relationships.

Japan has enjoyed a free economic system. Although not perfect, the political, economic, and social conditions are sufficient to guarantee free competition. In individual firms operating under these conditions, capital and management are generally separated, with the stockholders seldom exerting oppressive control over management. Since managers are not overly concerned with short-term profits, there is a good probability that they will act with a long-range point of view.

Most Japanese think of themselves as middle class, and so Japanese firms are made up of people with very little feeling of class differences. Management and workers are tied together by a sense of unity, which is very important in developing vitality in a firm. These two factors—the behavior of management based on a long-range point of view and a vitality that results from a human organization with little class consciousness—were very important in spurring the growth of the Japanese economy from postwar impoverishment to the present prosperity. They also brought Japan safely through such difficulties as the oil shocks.

ACHIEVING COMPETITIVENESS

Beginning in the 1960s, automobile output proceeded rapidly in Japan along with the sustained growth in the Japanese economy. Demand for private passenger cars spread quickly and production of vehicles grew from 480,000 to 5,290,000, more than tenfold in the ten years from 1960 to 1970. In 1980, the figure reached 11,040,000. The Japanese auto industry was forced to deal with tremendous production pressures.

Automobiles are made up of more than 10,000 parts, primarily made by related industries and groups of companies. Obtaining necessary parts, assembling them efficiently, and assuring quality at a reasonable price are naturally important issues. Efforts in this direction have been fostered with the industry itself.

First, a supply base was established for items such as tires, batteries, and springs, which have a widespread market. It was fairly easy to obtain enough of these parts for rapidly expanding needs, and cost advantages resulted from mass production. Of course, this was true for basic items like steel and paint as well. The automakers stimulated competition among parts firms by placing parallel orders for these parts and materials among several different suppliers. These specialized manufacturers developed the ability to compete internationally very quickly through interaction with both the automakers and interfirm competition.

Second, there was the problem of specialty parts, such as exterior and interior trim and body parts, which have a short model life and for which specifications differ by auto company. The automakers found it necessary to concentrate their human and material resources on major segments of the production process to expand their manufacturing capacity quickly. Therefore, in the early stages, they were forced to rely on small outside manufacturers with specialized technology even though they were weak and undeveloped. Some of these firms were run by individuals or families; many small companies could not handle mass production by their own efforts and their existence was precarious.

On the basis of a long-term policy the automakers took the initiative to develop these small manufacturers as affiliates of their own companies. They introduced production control techniques including work standards in the shops and factories. Then, they instituted scientific control technology, such as quality control (QC) based on statistical techniques. As a result of this, the gradual progress toward automation in plant and equipment, and the favorable conditions created by the vigorous demand for automobiles, these subcontracting firms grew in both scale and quality to develop a mass production capacity. The automakers gradually reduced the assistance given to these affiliated companies as they developed more strength and began to demand a more effective mass production system, better quality, and lower prices.

To meet these demands, it was no longer possible for the parts suppliers to simply use the drawings provided by the automaker to meet specifications. They had to become more independent and to develop the necessary technological expertise and cost-saving techniques to meet the automakers' design requirements. Suppliers were then able to expand their business beyond the automaker. Moreover, the competition between manufacturers in the same fields made the industry stronger and the competitive environment improved. Many of these affiliated suppliers have also become internationally competitive.

With the fierce worldwide competition in small cars in the 1980s, the parts makers are making a great effort to meet the demand for reductions in size and weight and improved performance. While keeping a close eye on new advances in technology at home and abroad, they are carrying out their own research and development in materials and electronics. New product development is constantly pursued to meet competition, and the parts makers are working actively to help the automakers with reduced costs. Japan currently has eleven automobile manufacturing firms, with price competition more intense than in the U.S. or Europe. In order to reach the target prices set for competitiveness in the marketplace, automakers and parts suppliers work together continually to reduce costs and work out changes in parts specifications. A price estimate not correctly based on costs will eventually break down. Price estimates are not generally accepted at face value. The automaker and parts supplier analyze the possible problems together and settle on a price acceptable to both sides. If increases in material or labor costs are directly reflected in the prices of parts or finished vehicles, the products will be quickly eliminated from the competition. Therefore, both sides must work together using all possible means to achieve rationalization.

PRODUCTION AND QUALITY CONTROL

In recent years, the requirements of automobile users have become more diverse and specialized. Advance production and large inventories may be used to meet these requirements without long delays, but this makes it difficult to maintain the cost minimum. A production system must be developed that makes it possible to fill orders promptly without maintaining a large inventory and without adversely affecting production. We are now using an order entry system (OES), in which the dealers, automakers, and parts suppliers are linked by computer to produce a highly responsive production schedule. Production is carried out smoothly with minimum inventory, and the automakers and parts suppliers work together to synchronize production. With this production control system, they cooperate to make the right quantity of the right product at the right time. The action plate method (APM) is an important part of this system, also called the *kanban* system in other companies.

Synchronization of the production process between the parts supplier and the automaker has a strong relationship with quality control. The synchronized system will not work unless the supplier's parts are 100% guaranteed for quality and can be directly delivered to the automaker without an acceptance inspection. Defective parts cannot be allowed in the auto production line. Therefore, it is necessary for the parts suppliers continually to improve their technical and control capability as well as the quality of the products themselves in order to gain the recognition necessary for survival in the competition. Quality and technology information exchanges with the automaker promote an understanding of the parts supplier's technological level, allowing for educational support. The automobile manufacturer also rewards QC to motivate suppliers to improve their QC systems.

OVERSEAS PROCUREMENTS

Because of the relationship between the automakers and parts suppliers, it is wrong to conclude that it is impossible to sell parts in Japan. Japanese automakers are constantly searching throughout the world for parts that are competitive in quality, technology, and price. They take such specific measures as creating departments to handle overseas procurement, sending purchasers overseas on permanent assignment, and organizing separate companies for this purpose. Japanese auto companies have made aggressive purchases of highly competitive parts that depend on abundant resources, such as aluminum, rubber, petrochemical materials, and cloth, and also of high-quality products that depend on superior technology, such as turbochargers, catalysts, lights, and tires. The direct purpose of these purchases is to improve the commercial competitiveness of Japan's products. The use of international sources of technology and materials also should stimulate domestic firms to increase their international competitiveness.

The source of the vitality maintained and exerted by firms related to the auto industry in Japan is the fierce domestic competition and the continuous effort required to grow in such an environment. Japanese automakers and affiliated parts suppliers must continue to understand and respect each other's position and to maintain and develop a functional relationship based on competition between suppliers. The most desirable results are produced in a free economy when free competition is preserved to the greatest extent possible. The lingering world recession has exacerbated the conflicts in world trade, and protectionist measures are being taken in Europe and the U.S. A retreat to protectionism will obstruct the healthy functioning of the market and allow industries to relax their efforts to improve their international competitiveness.

The Japanese auto industry also continues to contribute to the economies of its trading partners by technological collaboration with foreign manufacturers, joint ventures, and overseas investment, while it attempts to keep exports of finished cars at a level that will not create excessive economic problems. Japan is willing to participate in a spirit of healthy competition and cooperation, in a free economic system, to work for the long-term progress of the world auto industry and the overall prosperity of the world economy.

The "Active" Firm:
A Case Study of Nippon Kokan

MINORU KANAO

President
Nippon Kokan KK
Japan

DEFINITION OF AN "ACTIVE" ORGANIZATION

An enterprise's activity is comprised of the cooperative activity of the members who belong to the enterprise. Therefore, in order to increase the efficiency of the enterprise's activity, a large amount of cooperation and integrity of activity in the organization are indispensable. Formerly, the cooperative activity of the members was brought about by intensified control by the managers or the staff entrusted with this power. This system is typically called "scientific management."

In accordance with the principles of the scientific management system, workers at production sites were requested to do their work in strict conformity with the standard operating procedures set up by management. Namely, there had been clear job specifications: the planning function of management and the simple manual labor of the workers. The workers at work sites were thus prohibited from developing or expressing original ideas, and so the integrity of the organization was based on the policy of a few elite managers. This system was functioning well when the living standards of the whole society were relatively low and the desires of the average citizen were modest. However, problems arose as a more complex nation evolved.

As a result of remarkable economic growth after the end of World War II, people's living standards have grown tremendously and the fulfillment of their social requirements has become more important. For example, the majority of Japanese blue-collar workers are senior high school graduates. At this level of educational attainment, workers object to strict adherence to instructions issued by their superiors. The recent phenomena of increased rates of absenteeism and job transfers in many industrial nations may be manifestations of workers' resistance to bureaucratic management. A shift of emphasis from bureaucratic management to an "active" organization may help reduce dissatisfaction among personnel. In an active organization it is absolutely necessary that cooperation among the members is not forced but is voluntary. The achievement of the goals of the whole organization should mean the self-improvement of the individual members as well. To make an active organization is not a new problem, because harmony between the individual and the entire society is a perpetual issue that cannot easily be reconciled.

CASE EXAMPLES OF NIPPON KOKAN

Introduction of the Ogishima Complex

Nippon Kokan is an integrated, heavy industrial enterprise consisting of steel-making, shipbuilding, and engineering/construction, with four steel mills and three factories. Nippon Kokan employs about 35,000 workers, of which 11,000 are white-collar workers and 24,000 are blue-collar workers.

The oldest steel mill is situated in the industrial area halfway between Tokyo and Yokohama. Renovation of this mill began in 1969. This was a large-scale project, where new blast furnaces and other major facilities were constructed on a 1400-acre man-made island. The existing facilities were completely scrapped, and the "Ogishima complex" was completed in 1979. The construction was carried out under very difficult conditions. First, it was implemented during the slow economic growth period following the first oil crisis. Second, we had to follow the extremely strict regulations and laws regarding pollution that are stipulated for the highly populated areas of Tokyo and Yokohama.

The purpose of this renovation project was to seek the drastic realization of pollution-free operation and reduction of production costs. Consequently, ultra-modern technology and facilities were introduced with control systems and operation methods radically different from previous ones.

Active Participation of Workers at Ogishima

Plant operators were to be transferred from the old factories to the new one. A strategy to familiarize the workers with the new operating techniques of the highly automated plants posed a serious problem.

One of the major facilities is a hot strip mill, which continuously produces coil-shaped thin steel sheets by rolling flat steel ingots called slabs. About 10% of the 220 workers needed for this hot strip mill had been selected as "core workers" a year before the start of operation in 1978. They were assigned the job of assisting the engineers during the equipment installation phase. These core workers had learned the structure and operating principles of the equipment and facilities through the work assigned to them.

Having obtained complete understanding of the fundamentals of the equipment, they prepared the standard operating procedures as well as other types of manuals. Thus, these core workers became qualified to be instructors in plant operations.

Three months prior to the start of operation, 30% of the personnel were transferred to the new plant from the old one and were trained in the method of plant operation by the core workers. The remaining 60% were assigned to the new plant for the first time at the start of operation and were trained by the other 40% of previously trained workers on a man-to-man system, resulting in a smooth start for the operation of the plant.

Worker Participation in the Preparation of Standard Operating Procedures and Job Manuals

Although manuals were prepared by the core workers of the hot strip mill prior to initial start-up, review of the standard operating procedures and various kinds of manuals is done continuously. Front-line operators and maintenance men voluntarily participate. For instance, if a new problem occurs, they will prepare trouble-shooting manuals, which are integrated into a systematic and overall job manual. When necessary, of course, the engineers in the technical control department also contribute to the manual's preparation. They, as expert technicians, are in a position to give appropriate technical advice and assistance. A draft of the standard operating procedures drawn from discussions of the various groups will be finalized after approval by the superintendent. Items in the draft requiring further coordination with other departments are also discussed by the technical control staff.

Because the standard operating procedures are written by the workers, they are willing to conform to them, and whenever a defect is found in the manuals, they will take the initiative to improve it by every possible means. The details of operation at the work site are better understood by the operators themselves than by the engineers. Consequently, the operators have abundant ideas as to how the work procedures should be changed for higher efficiency. A proper environment of management systems in which the operators' ideas can be freely utilized leads directly to a marked improvement in managerial efficiency.

THE TRANSFORMATION FROM BLUE COLLAR TO WHITE COLLAR

It has often been said that at a stage when higher automation is realized, the work assigned to the workers will be simplified and will not require their judgment. However, according to the experience we have had so far, it is not true. As long as the equipment is operated normally, it seems that the operator has just to watch the instruments in the control room. It is common in an automated factory that a number of work processes are closely integrated, and because of this, a single problem in a certain part of the system will inevitably be compounded in many other processes. Therefore, it is important and necessary for the operators to understand completely the entire system for correct assessment of the situation and for appropriate communication. In this sense, we believe that the work of the operators in a highly automated factory is rather close to information processing.

As for the introduction of robots in a factory, we stress the policy that robots should be employed for monotonous and dangerous work in poor conditions, so that workers can perform work that is worthy of a human being.

One result of factory automation in Japan has been the transformation from blue-collar to white-collar work. In addition, the progressive rise in educational attainment has diminished blind obedience on the part of blue-collar workers in accepting the dictums of management. Great efforts have been made to eliminate blue-collar discrimination, and the system is very suitable to the present level of technological innovation. Nippon Kokan's horizontal system gives all employees the opportunity to be transferred from blue-collar to white-collar work or promoted to managerial positions. Employees enjoy the status of equal treatment within the company.

LABOR UNIONS AND THE WAGE SYSTEM

The harmony among blue- and white-collar workers also appears in the organization of Japan's labor unions. The present labor unions comprise both categories of workers. Following a process of severe confrontation between management and workers immediately after World War II, the labor unions had demanded the elimination of various inequities between workers, thus gradually realizing the present state of lesser discrimination.

For example, wage differences exist among Japanese manufacturers, and the engineers earn 20% more than the operators. The principle for determining the wage of blue-collar workers is very similar to that of white-collar workers, and the wage levels of the two are relatively close. If we take a look at the example of Nippon Kokan, the wage system, excluding that of management, for both white- and blue-collar workers is exactly the same; and their wages are mainly determined by what the employee knows, what he can do, and how his ability is utilized in performing his work.

Besides wages, Nippon Kokan provides health and welfare programs equally to white- and blue-collar workers. For instance, both college graduate engineers and high school graduate operators live together in the same dormitories for single employees.

EFFICIENT COMMUNICATION

Finally, there is the emphasis on communication. In Japanese enterprises, the front-line operators are required to use their independent judgment. In order for them to make proper decisions, it is necessary to keep them well informed on managerial matters. In the case of Nippon Kokan, a full three-month training program is given to newly employed operators, and a one-year program to those employed as maintenance men.

The major aim in this series of training is for the employees to acquire technical abilities directly related to the performance of the duty assigned. They are also given instructions about the work processes that come before and after their own assigned duty and an opportunity to observe these facilities for themselves. Moreover, they are taught the company history, the problems the company faces, and relationships with the competitors.

Besides the training for the new employees, there are also various types of training for engineers, administrative staffs, and managers within the company. This becomes an important channel through which the company's policy, as well as the policy of the top personnel, is directly conveyed to the employees. Information is also conveyed through the periodicals that the company publishes. Particular emphasis is focused on the new year's address delivered to the employees by the president as an essential communications' vehicle. A management–labor conference that is held at least quarterly is also an important means of dialogue. We are always trying to make full use of as many channels as possible, whether formal or informal, so that as much information as possible may be conveyed to the employees.

Concerning the effect of managerial information, it has been said that those who are positive in their attitudes toward management and who have high motivation in their work are inclined to accept managerial information positively, but on the contrary those who have a negative attitude accept it negatively. This tendency makes it all the more important that we carry out policies such as better treatment for the workers along with the conveyance of necessary information, in order to create a positive attitude among the employees. Removal of discrimination between the blue- and white-collar workers is one of the major steps in winning employees' confidence to react favorably to the information that flows from management.

Finally, an active organization can be realized only in a system based upon a philosophy that all the employees are equally important *partners* for successful management.

Index